The Language of Social Casework

LIBRARY OF SOCIAL WORK

GENERAL EDITOR: NOEL TIMMS

Lecturer in Social Science and Administration
London School of Economics

The Language of Social Casework

by Noel Timms

Lecturer in Social Science and Administration
London School of Economics

LONDON

ROUTLEDGE & KEGAN PAUL

NEW YORK: HUMANITIES PRESS

First published 1968
by Routledge & Kegan Paul Ltd
Broadway House, 68-74 Carter Lane
London, E.C.4

Printed in Great Britain
by Northumberland Press Limited
Gateshead

SBN 7100 6204 4 C
SBN 7100 6214 1 P

General editor's introduction

The Library of Social Work is designed to meet the needs of students following courses of training for social work. In recent years the number and kinds of training in Britain have increased in an unprecedented way. But there has been no corresponding increase in the supply of textbooks to cover the growing differentiation of subject matter or to respond to the growing spirit of enthusiastic but critical enquiry into the range of subjects relevant to social work. The Library will consist of short texts designed to introduce the student to the main features of each topic of enquiry, to the significant theoretical contributions so far made to its understanding, and to some of the outstanding problems. Each volume will suggest ways in which the student might continue his work by further reading.

This book begins by considering the way in which social workers commonly neglect language, their own and other people's. It is suggested that part of this neglect is due to the ways in which social workers and their critics envisage the activity of social work. The traditional criticisms of philanthropy and social work are, therefore, reviewed, and an attempt made to describe some common responses to

v

them on the part of the practitioners. This is followed by an examination of two terms that are of some importance in the language of casework; the 'generic-specific' concept, and the idea of the 'settings' of casework. But casework is also described in terms borrowed from other contexts: it is seen as 'art' or as 'science', as a 'therapy' or the offer of 'friendship'. Each of these descriptions is considered in the last two chapters of the book.

This study differs to some extent from other volumes in the Library. It is not a detailed account of work in a specialised field of social work nor a study of one particular aspect of social work theory or practice. The questions raised in this volume are of a general kind, though they have implications for the more specialised treatment of the different elements into which social work is usually divided. It will soon be apparent that the present volume attempts to introduce a crucial theme by examining a number of topics which are in themselves complex. The chapter on the concepts of the 'generic' and 'specific' in social work, for example, refers to quite difficult and rather abstract questions, whilst that on social work as science or art cannot avoid questions concerning the nature of 'science' and 'art'. These questions, it is argued, are directly relevant to an understanding of social work, but they cannot, of course, be exhaustively treated in this book. This qualification applies throughout the present work; it will not be repeated in each chapter, but should be borne in mind. The questions that arise will be treated in a way that indicates the nature of the problem and also the next steps in a possible argument. Quotations have been used with deliberate liberality to establish as fully as possible the relevance of a fairly wide range of sources and to indicate with some precision useful further reading. More questions will be raised than questions answered, and some of the uncertainties exposed are not capable of a ready solution. Nor would a ready-made solution necessarily be the most helpful, since a recognition of the uncertainty and its patient exploration is more likely to help us to understand the nature of social work.

NOEL TIMMS

Contents

1
Introduction

The neglect of language

It is surprising that social workers, who are so largely dependent on language, should have given such little attention to words and to what it means to speak a language. Their activity has been described as the attempt to cure through talk, and their case records contain in summary or verbatim form accounts of innumerable conversations with their clients. A significant part of social work training seems to consist in the correct appreciation of a group of key terms, such as 'acceptance', 'self-determination' and so on, and the literature of social work seems concerned to repeat (rather than articulate) a particular verbal tradition. Yet social workers pay little attention to language, their own or other people's. At present they seem preoccupied with questions concerning their role in society; should they, for instance, *progress* from being 'therapists' to becoming 'reformers'. Such questions cannot be satisfactorily answered, since no one has yet considered how we can recognise 'an advance' in social work.

It is true that from time to time social workers will remind themselves or be reminded of the importance of the careful definition of terms, of 'being precise', but a great deal can be said with the assistance of the most rudimentary definition, and 'precision' is a meaningless objective outside the context of a particular language. Alternatively, social workers occasionally attack or defend what is described as the 'use of jargon' (Butler, 1962; Anderson, 1964), but jargon is commonly seen as either otiose or a matter of the straightforward borrowing of terms from another vocabulary rather than a reference to a whole way of seeing things outside the confines of social work. Thus, a social worker might complain that such commonly used phrases as 'relationship is the worker's main tool' or 'the worker uses the interview as a tool' were simply long-winded ways of referring to the importance of relationships and the interview: that the reference to 'tools' was unnecessary. Such criticism would, however, overlook a possible clue to an advance in our understanding of social work; it fails to see that 'tool talk' is a particular way of talking, with certain implications. To describe something as a tool is to say that it is, to some extent, 'graspable', that one can inspect it, that it is designed for a particular job, so that one can see when it is in need of repair, and judge when a better model appears on the market, and so on. So, when the social work interview is described as a 'tool', it is thereby given 'tool-like' attributes whose effectiveness as helpful or otherwise in advancing our understanding of social work activity must be assessed.

Language does not occupy a central place in social work, and social workers themselves appear indifferent to its significance. It is worth enquiring why. Two factors can readily be identified: their mistrust of language, and their apparent belief that it is somehow dispensable.

Language as distortion, and dispensable

Many social work writers seem to experience language as an external force which distorts social work activity. Thus, Biestek (1961, p. viii) in a much used text suggests that social workers have been inarticulate in explaining the casework relationship because 'no explanation or definition can do justice to a living thing; words have a certain coldness, while relationship has a delightful warmth.' Yet definitions and explanations could be said to be judged to be more or less adequate according to the extent to which they do *justice* to a living thing, and whilst words can be said to have colour they are not usually described as having warmth or coldness. Another writer complains of efforts 'to force into the mold of logical and watertight definition that which defies every attempt to define', and claims that the process of casework 'can be known in ways far more reliable than words alone afford' (Faatz, 1953, p. 5 and p. 7). It is difficult to see what meaning can be given to 'words alone', and how we can test the reliability of what cannot be stated. In social work writing words tend either to be used with ill-considered liberality, thus giving Wootton and other critics the opportunity of a harvest of literal nonsense, or to be abandoned in favour of communication through experience, because of the seemingly impossible demands of 'watertight' definitions. Both tendencies neglect the essential part played by language in structuring our experience.

Social workers in training are often encouraged not to accept 'at face value' what their clients say, and to see themselves as 'getting behind' the words the clients use. The words are seen as a disguise, the significance of which is exhausted once it has been penetrated. The crucial objective is envisaged as lying *beyond* rather than *in* words, and at the centre of the activity lies 'the intuitive spark and feel for the heart of social casework as a process in human relationship'. (Smalley, 1967, p. 21.) It is possible to detect within this approach the view that in social work relationships language becomes sooner or later dispensable. Such a view, quite widely held though with different emphases, undervalues the role of language and the part social work can play in the exploration of emotion as a social activity.

Language plays a critical part in the constitution of our social life, not simply in its description. This is true whether we are concerned with public relationships, with those of a more intimate nature, or with what can be described as a man's relationship with himself. As Herder observed (quoted Barnard, 1965, p. 57), 'language is the medium through which man becomes conscious of his inner self and at the same time it is the key to the understanding of his outer relationships. It unites him with, but also differentiates him from, others.' The place of language in the creation and maintenance of human relations has been ably explored by Cornforth (1965) in a study of Marxist philosophy and what is often described as linguistic analysis. Certainly, the relationships social workers form with their clients are always seen as important, but they are often described as if they had somehow a life of their own which was 'beyond' words. Language, however, plays a crucial role in human relations of all kinds. Cornforth (*ibid.*, p. 308) goes so far as to assert that 'they could not exist unless spoken into existence . . . human bodies do not enter into human relations independently of what they say and think, so that language has more to do with these relations than simply to state them as facts. It is only by using language that people enter into them.'

4

The idea that language is dispensable, and perhaps that it ought sometimes to be dispensed with in favour of some kind of communication through feeling, also detracts from the important role social work can play in the task of describing feelings. It is sometimes objected that social workers are preoccupied with feelings, their own or those of their clients. Professor Titmuss (1965), for example, has suggested that 'Research workers retire to cultivate their ten square inches of social phenomena for much the same reason that caseworkers continually re-examine their feelings about dominant mothers and passive fathers. . . . They are all looking for a haven of security and neutrality in which to protect and perfect their professional souls in an increasingly complex and changing world.' Social workers might defensively reply that their feelings about their clients played an important part in the treatment. Yet the challenge itself should be examined. Security and neutrality is not what would normally be expected to follow from a 're-examination' of feelings, and the continuous kind of critical activity envisaged could be seen as serving an important social function. As Hampshire (1960, p. 65) has observed, 'moods, states of mind, feelings and sensations have to be described, the particular quality of them communicated; and to find more and more effective ways of describing them is the most serious of all the necessary refinements of language. It is serious because moods, states of mind and feelings must be distinguished and identified in a society before they can be facts that enter into man's practical intentions and manners.'

Other languages

We have been concerned with substantiating an incon-

gruity—the social worker's lack of systematic critical
attention to language when words play such a crucial
role in both social work education and practice. So far attention has been paid to what might be called the language of social work, but in expounding and developing
their work social workers also refer to other languages.
They sometimes, for instance, look for a social work
philosophy, or they describe their work as an *art* or a
science. These references are not usually successful, and
they appear to suffer from two main faults. They ignore
problems in the realms of discourse to which they refer,
and they fail to take seriously the several different kinds
of activity that constitute social work.

The first failure can most easily be illustrated from the
treatment usually accorded to 'social work values'. This
subject receives attention in almost every book on social
work, and the values most commonly cited include respect
for the individual, self-determination, acceptance and inter-
dependence. These seem to be held in something of a
vacuum, and if they are placed at all, it is in the limitless
space of 'democracy' or 'Christianity'. Thus, Hamilton
(1949) states that 'the method of social casework . . .
cannot be isolated from the democratic frame of reference
and culture within which it has developed'. Again, Towle
(1954, p. 364) writes 'As the basic concepts and working
principles of casework are presented and discussed, they
are identified as old, in that they are the basic tenets of
democracy as a way of life. . . . We are concerned that
social casework be a democratic helping process.' Statements like these, common in social work writing, seem to
assume that 'democracy' has only one meaning that can be
considered legitimate. They fail to see that the term is
itself problematic. Macpherson (1965), for example, has

recently shown that liberal democracy, and its Communist and its underdeveloped variants, can all be legitimately described as democratic. Have social work values a particular connection with all or only one or two of these democratic forms of government?

Similarly, statements are frequently made connecting social work values with Christianity. Modern social work is said to have originated in Christian values and to be a current expression of them. Both statements require much more exploratory work before they can be rightfully made. The first must take account of the fact that social work in the formative period of the late nineteenth century was often seen as a substitute for Christian religious practice and belief. The second statement must be reconciled with the fact that the denial of what has seemed to be central Christian doctrine is sometimes assumed to provide a basis for contemporary social work practice. Thus, a recent publication lists as one of the basic principles of professional social work: 'To understand that the behaviour of an individual is not due to original sin or to perversity, but is explicable in terms of the individual in the course of his development.' (*A Socialist View of Social Work.*) This gives, of course, no idea of the complexity or the development of Christian teaching on original sin, so that we cannot know what is being denied. Moreover, it ignores the fact that behaviour can be understood in many different ways. It is difficult to see why 'perversity' is ruled out from the start as a satisfactory explanation for at least some purposes. It is important to recognise that a situation can be explained in a number of different ways, and that we choose between them according to the purpose in hand. This, however, is not the point at which textual criticism should be elaborated. The main purpose in citing the two attempts to connect social work with other languages—the political and the religious—has been to suggest that they fail because they do not recognise controversy in the realms of discourse to which they refer. They borrow terms without trying to understand the full and special meaning they possess in another linguistic context.

Attempts to place social work in a wider context than that supplied by its own operations have also been marked by a failure to study the ways in which social workers have described their separate activities. Instead, the attempt has been made to characterise all social work as, for instance, an art or a science. This is not a productive approach. We should not, at this stage at any rate, be asking a wholesale question like, What is social work? Rather we should be more patiently following the implications of the ways in which social workers describe their activities. For example, social workers quite often compile what they term a 'social history'. Does this resemble writing the history of a particular person or family? If it does, what counts as an accurate history, and how does the worker understand someone historically? Again, social workers make judgements about people: they judge that some clients are, for instance, immature, unco-operative and so on. They also claim that they avoid condemning people. This seems to be a special position, but it perhaps resembles the stance that the literary critic tries to maintain in appraising the maturity and intelligence of an author, or his degree of self-knowledge (Robson, 1966).

As a final illustration, we can take the idea of understanding which occupies a valued place in social work. When a social worker tells a client that he 'understands' does this resemble the situation in which a scientist grasps the results of an experiment, or a literary critic judges that a novel is 'true to life', or an historian claims to see the significance of the murder of Becket? Alternatively, what makes us question a social worker's understanding? When we say that a social worker's interpretation of his client's behaviour is 'far-fetched', are we making the same kind of statement as an historian confronted with the view that Becket's murder was in fact a ritual sacrifice, or as a literary critic assessing the claim that James Joyce's *Ulysses* closely follows the pattern of the Roman mass?

It is a comment on social work education that questions like this will appear strange or 'unreal' within a social work context. They are posed not from perversity, but as part of the necessary attempt to 'place' social work activity, to make it intelligible, and to convey some of the intellectual excitement that should accompany the exploration of its problems. Previous attempts to identify social work have met with only modest success because they have ignored problems of language. Social work has been explored in terms that are exclusively 'professional' or in terms whose wider frame of reference has not been appreciated. Many people, for example, could envisage taking a particular problem to a child care officer, to a probation officer, a psychiatric social worker and so on, but they would be puzzled at the idea of a social worker. Social workers themselves would probably argue that these particular occupations are based on a complex of knowledge, attitude and skill which is 'generic' to social work. They would claim that social work is a recognisable activity carried out in a variety of organisations which constitute the 'settings' of practice. Yet the idea of 'generic' knowledge, attitude and skill is not, as we shall see, immediately clear, and carries implications which are seldom recognised. Similarly, social work is described as an 'art'

or a 'science', as 'therapy' or 'friendship', but the significance of these claims is rarely exploited, their implications
seldom grasped.

These attempts to identify social work, which will be
discussed in detail in the following chapters, indicate that
social work is an activity worthy of imaginative and
serious study. Yet, today this is not the predominant impression to be gained from either practitioners or their
critics, who maintain attitudes that the next chapter will
attempt to describe as traditional. The practitioner is unsure
of his place in the hierarchy of status and on the map of
intellectual activity. He tends to see the solution to this
problem in terms of the advancement of his profession and
the search for more empirical data on clients and social
workers, their problems, their attitudes to help and so on.
In this perspective language has its uses in advancing the
profession, and making statistics intelligible. The critics,
on the other hand, tend to discount the language of social
work, seeing it as nothing more than camouflage either for
professional claims (Wootton, 1955) or for good intentions
(Halmos, 1965). The approach adopted in this book will be
to take the language of social work seriously, but to begin
to study and consider its implications. It is based on the
general conviction that social work education has, to
borrow words from another context, so far made too little
'provision for teaching people how to be ignorant'. (Oakeshott, 1962, p. 308.)

2
Critics and practitioners

Social workers tend to take themselves and their activities very seriously, but it is not always easy for those outside the occupation to see why they should do likewise. For many 'social work' is a term that combines the dedication and ambiguity of 'social' with ordinary, straightforward 'work'. It seems a necessary, even a worthy task, but not one capable of sustaining much curiosity or requiring careful and imaginative exploration. A common attitude towards social work is represented in one of Kingsley Amis' characters (in *My Enemy's Enemy*), who supposes that social workers are necessary, but wonders if they have to behave 'like a kind of revivalist military policeman'. Practitioners of social work, on the other hand, have not found it easy to describe their work in ways that are theoretically or imaginatively compelling. This chapter will consider some of the reasons why social work is both so little regarded and so elusive.

The position of social work

To some extent social workers are themselves to blame.

Like students of social administration they have often espoused a cause where they should have attempted to explore a meaning. For example, teachers of social work have tended to occupy important positions in the struggle to attain widespread recognition of social work as a profession. This has hindered the exploration of at least two important facets of professionalism. In the first place, it seems possible in contemporary society to be professional in a number of ways. When professional status is claimed by and for social workers, are we claiming that they are professional in the same way as doctors or as engineers or as librarians? The issue of the professional status of social work will be the subject of another volume in this library, but if we consider the last possibility it is worth noting a recent discussion on 'Professions and Non-Professions' (Goode, 1966). This suggested that the librarian had failed to develop a general body of scientific theory bearing on the problem of the choice of, and appropriate access to, sources of information, and, equally significant, the public did not recognise any difference between a professional and a non-professional librarian. The librarian, like other groups of workers, had moved in the direction of professionalism, but he still responded to the expressed desires of people rather than to their needs. This brief reference to the professionalism of groups other than social workers is sufficient to indicate some of the problems that are likely to be ignored in the pursuit of professional status.

A second group of problems also likely to receive less attention than they deserve are those connected with the possible adverse effects of achieved professional status. A professional is, for instance, a man who has succeeded in creating a certain social distance between himself and other members of his society. He is committed to increasing both the intrinsic and the extrinsic rewards of his own specialised occupation. In other words, we cannot assume that the meaning of being a professional in our society can be considered in only positive terms. This was vividly illustrated on a small scale when at a conference on 'The Concept of Professional Status' (1957) a speaker remarked, 'I think whenever the affairs of a profession are discussed in public, that profession loses a little of its prestige.' Those who are interested in promoting a particular professional cause, however, are unlikely to give lengthy consideration to the negative aspects of professionalism. They are also likely to assume that groups of workers can become professional only by following the example of one favoured group that has already achieved unquestionable status, as, for example, doctors.

Yet, whilst social workers strive for future professional status, they also occupy a place in present society. Some have argued that their position in society at least helps to explain the twin failures to expound and accept the nature of social work. It has been suggested, for example, that social workers have 'to affirm and implement moral and social values to which society itself may give only contradictory or partial expression and support' (Rapoport, 1960). The author goes on to argue that social workers may be seen as a reminder of society's failure, and as members of a minority group both tolerated and feared. 'The social work profession is trying to find its boundaries in a period of culture change while it simultaneously is charged by society to contribute to the furtherance of profound social changes.' These possibilities would clearly repay investigation, but the terms used tend to combine analysis and prescription; they are part of a language (e.g. 'society's failures', 'charged by society') which should be accepted at its exchange rather than its face value.

Yet the main weight of a reply to the question concerning the elusiveness of social work will probably come from an analysis of the traditions of philanthropy and of the criticism of philanthropy. The faults that contemporary critics find in social work closely resemble those discovered in earlier philanthropists, whilst the response of the modern social worker also follows an earlier pattern. The remaining sections of this chapter will be concerned with elucidating these traditions. Their exploration will begin to remove some of the difficulties that often deprive general discussions of social work of much of their potential interest and advantage.

The criticism of philanthropy and social work

The philanthropist and his successor the social worker have often had a bad press. In order to understand this largely negative response we should consider the development of three terms, charity, philanthropy and social work. An adequate study of these terms would constitute the modern history of charity which we require and which was attempted from a late nineteenth-century perspective by C. S. Loch (1910). Such a comprehensive treatment is not possible in the present volume, and all that can be attempted is a sketch of the main elements in the poor reputation accorded to philanthropy and social work since the nineteenth century.

The failure of the rich to live up to their responsibilities to the poor has been a subject for literature and for exhortation from very early times. Piers Plowman, for example, in the fourteenth century severely criticised the rich for failing to grasp the practical implications of their brotherhood with the poor. This, however, was not the criticism voiced against the philanthropist as the role began to emerge distinctly in the eighteenth century. The philanthropist was not, in fact, necessarily wealthy, but he was seen and perceived himself as a specialist in welfare, someone who directly pursued the objective of 'doing good'. The philanthropist was not a person who did good almost incidentally because he had become a good squire, or a responsible landlord. He was someone who sought status through specialised philanthropic activities. This attitude, which had no place in the world of Piers Plowman, is well illustrated in a nineteenth-century context in De Melun's discussion on friendly societies with Louis Napoleon, who 'insisted much on the advantage of uniting in this work the different social classes, through admitting the well-to-do as honorary members, and the workers as participating members' (quoted Vidler, 1964, p. 61). Gradually, the philanthropist gained an unfavourable reputation. He was pictured as gullible, easily led to accept accounts of behaviour of which others would be more sceptical; he was narrow-minded, in the sense of pursuing very limited goals without conspicuous intelligence; he was intrusive and insensitive, and it was difficult to know which was the more sinister, his attempts to pry or his infrequent moments of triumphant 'understanding'. Above all the motives of the philanthropist became suspect; his philanthropy concealed more than it donated.

This composite picture of the philanthropist is, of course, a reconstruction which ignores the favourable impressions of the philanthropist on a small scale: the man, or more usually woman, who 'did good' unobtrusively, like the relatives of clergymen recorded in many of the Victorian novels. There were, for instance, the two sisters of Mr. Irwine in *Adam Bede* whom 'no one ever thought of mentioning . . . except the poor people in Braxton village, who regarded them as deep in the science of medicine, and spoke of them vaguely as "the gentlefolk". If any one had asked old Dummilow who gave him his flannel jacket he would have answered, "the gentlefolk, last winter"; and widow Steene dwelt much on the virtues of the "stuff" the gentlefolks gave her for her cough.'

Yet the shortcomings of the professional 'do-gooder' are well established in literature and in contemporary comment. The gullibility of the philanthropist, which can be currently illustrated by the contention that social workers are 'soft' both in their refusal to see that hard cases make bad law and in their reliance on fragile theories to understand themselves and others, is clearly visible in the original Lady Bountiful. She has come to represent almost anything that can be considered objectionable in philanthropy or social work, but this is to abuse her original character. The first Lady Bountiful, a character in Farquhar's *The Beaux' Stratagem*, appears in a humane rather than superior guise. She seems to rebuke Mrs. Sullen for being 'merry with the misfortunes of other people'; her misfortunes should teach her to pity others. Mrs. Sullen responds to this criticism by questioning Lady Bountiful's claim to 'have done miracles about the country with my receipts'.

> Mrs. Sullen : Miracles indeed, if they have cured anybody; but I believe, madam, the patient's faith goes farther towards the miracle than your prescription.
> Lady Bountiful : Fancy helps in some cases; but there's your husband who has as little fancy as anybody. I brought him from death's door.

Lady Bountiful is not generously endowed with intelligence, but in this she is scarcely conspicuous amongst the other characters in the play. The picture of the unintelligent philanthropist can be found fully developed in Manzoni's novel, *The Betrothed*, in the character of Donna Prassede. She is an old lady with a strong propensity to do good:

> certainly the worthiest profession that man can ply, but one which, like all others, is open to abuse. To do good one must know what it is; and like everyone else, we can only know this by means of our own passions, our own judgements, our own ideas—which often do not amount to very much. Donna Pressede's attitude towards ideas was the same as they say one should have towards friends; she had few but she was strongly attached to the few she had.

Amongst the ideas she held was 'a vague presumption that those who go beyond duty can also go beyond their rights'. This unquestioning, intrusive character is the distinguishing mark of a more famous English fictional character of about this time. Readers of *Bleak House* may recall Mrs. Pardiggle, whom Dickens described as 'a woman of rapacious benevolence' and who described herself in the following exhaustive manner: 'I am a School lady, I am a Visiting lady, I am a Reading lady, I am a distributing lady. I am on the local Linen Box Committee and many general committees.'

There seems to be much in common between the criticism Dickens intended of Mrs. Pardiggle and her kind and that made by Virginia Woolf of two near contemporary philanthropists, Canon and Mrs. Barnett.

I meant to write about the Barnetts and the peculiar

repulsiveness of those who dabble self-approvingly in the stuff of others' souls. The Barnetts were at any rate plunged to the elbow, red-handed if ever philanthropists were, which makes them good examples; and then un-questioning and unspeculative as they were, they give themselves away almost to the undoing of my critical faculty. Is it chiefly intellectual snobbery that makes me dislike them? Is it snobbery to feel outraged when she says 'Then I came close to the Great Gates'—or reflects that God=good, devil=evil. Has this coarseness of grain any necessary connection with labour for one's kind? And then the smug vigour of their self-satisfaction! Never a question as to the right of what they do—always a kind of insensate forging ahead until, naturally, their undertakings are all of a colossal size and portentous prosperity. (Woolf, 1953)

The philanthropist and social worker are seen, accord-ing to the tradition we are examining, as essentially un-critical of their own activities. They make claims on behalf of their work that cannot be sustained in any reflective manner. Sometimes the claims are seen as merely absurd. As Virginia Woolf wrote, 'the tale is made to unfold into full-blown success, like some profuse peony' (Woolf, *op. cit.*). At other times the claims appear more sinister. A sustained critical note in left-wing appraisals of philan-thropy and social work in the present century has centred around the claim 'to understand'. From Kirkman Gray (1908) to Baroness Wootton (1955) this has seemed to be a combination of technical and moral impossibilities. Kirk-man Gray stated that whilst we could give the widow financial help we could not enquire into her feelings about her condition. His 'could not' carried a double implica-tion: it was not possible to conduct such enquiry, and, even if it were, we ought not to try. Precisely these implications are to be found in Wootton's more recent and trenchant comment that in order to reach the level of understanding of her client seemingly required of the social worker, the worker would have to marry the client.

Left-wing criticism is also clearly apparent when we consider the final characterisation of philanthropy, that it is merely a device to conceal unworthy motives. The view that philanthropy or social work represents a personal or a group ideology would seem to suggest the influence of Freud and Marx respectively. It has been argued, for example, that

> the early literature of social work contains much evidence of the struggle to walk this narrow way between the Scylla of over-indulgence (based on guilt towards the deprived and the outcast) and the Charybdis of self-righteous contempt for the 'undeserving' (based on paranoid anxieties about the danger of unstable exploitation by these damaged clients). (Irvine, 1956)

Similarly, the view that philanthropists and social workers are simply serving class interests by attempting to support an essentially unstable and corrupt society has been the stock-in-trade of one particular group of critics since the late nineteenth century at least. Yet, the idea that philanthropic motives are often if not usually distorted can be found in writers before Marx and Freud, and in those not conspicuously influenced by either. Coleridge (1917, p. 261) for instance, wrote in 1833,

> 'I have never known a trader in philanthrophy who was not wrong in the heart somewhere or other. Individuals so distinguished are usually unhappy in their family

relations—men not benevolent or beneficent to individuals, but almost hostile to them, yet lavishing money and labour and time on the race, the abstract notion.

In the present century Virginia Woolf (1953) wrote that 'these social reformers and philanthropists get so out of hand and harbour so many discreditable desires under the disguise of loving their kind, that in the end there's more to find fault with in them than in us.' To this response to the potential rebuke of the philanthropist she added, however, the perceptive question, 'But if I were one of them?' The idea of Virginia Woolf as a moral welfare worker or a probation officer is not merely faintly amusing, it could also prove instructive.

The attitudes of practitioners

The question, 'if I were one of them', is significant. If taken seriously it would lead possibly to some modification in what has been outlined as a possible portrait of philanthropy. It would certainly place the critic in a position from which he could begin to consider why philanthropy has attracted such a consistent response. A simple answer to this question would be that philanthropists and, later, social workers have deserved such portraiture. The picture we can compile of their character is simply a reflection of their activities. There are two senses in which this could be said to be a reasonable view to adopt. Firstly, we can find many examples of the behaviour of philanthropists which accurately match the picture we have drawn. Mrs. Vicars, for instance, in charge of a Home for Female Penitents in the second half of the nineteenth century, returns a letter sent to one of the girls beginning, 'My very dear girl', and ending 'your affectionate sister'. In the matron's view the girl 'had no right to terms of affection such as would belong to a good girl or one struggling under a deep sense of her sin.' (Hopkins, 1874) Secondly, philanthropists and social workers are responsible for any distortions in the picture because of a failure to take seriously the task of exploring and explaining their own activity. This involves examining, albeit briefly, the other aspect of attitudes towards philanthropy and social work mentioned earlier, namely the attitudes of those engaged in either activity.

The attitudes of practitioners of philanthropy and social work towards their activity are, of course, complex, and in this section only those elements will be discussed which appear prominent in accounting for difficulties in communicating to others the kinds of activity philanthropists and social workers pursue. There seem to be two main elements: an emphasis on the practical at the expense of theorising, and what can be termed a doctrine of verbal inadequacy. The second factor has already been discussed in Chapter 1, and will be only briefly considered.

Initially the practitioners did not consider their activities to be very mysterious. The *Rules and Regulations of the Society for Bettering the Condition of the Poor at Clapham* (1817), for example, suggest that the basic problem is to reproduce in market towns and populous villages the social relationships between rich and poor characteristic of the small country village where 'the character and circumstances of every cottager are in general thoroughly known to any opulent person resident in it:—he naturally becomes the patron and friend of the poor—they look to him for advice, protection and relief:—a bond of union is formed between them equally honourable to the one, and

beneficial to the other.' To re-create this kind of relationship in more urbanised areas the 'opulent' should unite:
'by the money of one, the knowledge of another, the
zealous activity of a third, the discretion and patient per-
severance of a fourth, thrown into one common stock,
far more might be effected than could possibly be done by
the most strenuous exertions of an individual.' What is
uppermost in this account of philanthropic activity is the
simple co-ordination of untutored talents: if only certain
natural qualities could be combined welfare goals could be
achieved. The ideal of co-ordination persists into the nineteenth century and provides one of the main motives for
the foundation of the Charity Organisation Society, as
the very name suggests. 'Individualism' could perhaps describe one of the main objectives of this and other move-
ments of the time in so far as the treatment of cases of
hardship were concerned, but individualistic philanthropy
should not be allowed to 'run riot in all voluntary effort' as
Rathbone observed in a book originally entitled *Method
versus Muddle in Charitable Work* (1897).

Philanthropy and social work were thus seen as comparatively simple activities, and in so far as models were
sought these were found in such normal everyday relationships as those in the family or existing between master and
servant. As Octavia Hill suggested 'If the gentlefolk in the
neighbourhood would go down and turn over the pages
(of case records)—the sadder for their brevity—and just
ask themselves, if they were father or brothers in the
families of which they read, what they would suggest as
the wisest course; whether indeed, there was nothing for
it but weekly doles—no daughter who could go to service,
no plan by which effort and wisdom might raise the family
to independence, I think their extended education and out-

look might suggest some satisfactory plan in almost every case.' (quoted Bosanquet, 1914, p. 43). Social workers now accept more sophisticated models, though the use of ideas of immaturity still encourages the playing of parental roles towards at least certain clients. Yet the social worker still emphasises the practical activity at the expense of conceptual enquiry. There is still considerable support for the notion canvassed at the beginning of the century by one of the early university teachers of social work: 'If anything must go, let it be lectures and books, not the opportunities of gaining experience and taking a personal share for a time in constructive schemes for social reform.' (Macadam, 1914) 'Theory' and 'practice' are key terms in the development of social work, and their changing relationship constitutes the object of an enquiry in its own right. What can be stated here is the failure to grasp the intimate connection between the two. There is an instructive parallel with the way in which 'thought' and 'feeling' have been treated in social work. 'Thought' and 'feeling' have been separated so that intellectual activity could ultimately submit to feelings. Social workers in fact sometimes comment that in an interview many tactical mistakes might be made but the interview could nonetheless be successful 'because the worker's feeling was right'. Similarly, 'theory' has been divorced from 'practice', either to secure the primacy of practical considerations or to clothe practice in respectable garments. This separation of 'theory' and 'practice' has two related consequences. Firstly, 'practice' is distorted if it is conceived as simply a matter of applying 'theory' or even of applying 'theories', and 'theory' is misread if it is seen as some kind of summary of 'practice'. Secondly, we miss recognition of the conceptual connection between 'theory' and 'practice'.

We cannot conceive of practice without employing some kind of theory about what constitutes the practice, what indicates good or bad practice and so on. Circular argument often arises when, in answer to a question about the nature of social work activity, the social worker replies that this cannot be known unless the enquirer participates in the activity. 'Doing' is finally wrenched apart from 'describing', and no one apparently recognises the importance of the question that should follow the above interchange: how do I know when I am 'doing' it correctly; how do I know when I get it right?

In the last resort social workers complain, as we have seen, of the inadequacy of language. The relationships they form with clients, the emotional nuance of complex interactions defy description: they can only be communicated through experience. This kind of approach misrepresents communication, which 'is essentially the deliberate manifestation of an attitude towards a proposition or thinkable state of affairs' (Kneale, 1962). It also suggests that words can be inadequate in only one way. What requires examination is the kind of inadequacy thought to reside in words applied to social work. A word like 'relationship' for instance, should be seen not so much as inadequate as inexhaustible.

So far we have considered some of the obstacles to thinking of social work as an activity worthy of serious and imaginative study. These obstacles have been considered in the context of long-standing attitudes on the part of both critics and practitioners. We shall now review the ways in which certain key terms and ideas have been treated by social workers, and the remaining chapters of the book will be devoted to an examination of what it means to claim that casework is 'generic'; that casework and the setting in which it is practised are inseparably linked; that social work is scientific, and that it differs significantly from psychotherapy and from friendship. In discussing these separate but important questions it is hoped to advance the task of placing social work outlined in the first part of this chapter.

3
Generic and specific

Introduction—a question of meaning

Discussions of social work usually include, often at an early stage, some reference to the 'generic' nature of social work and to the specific application of 'generic' principles or knowledge. These related terms, 'generic' and 'specific', have been frequently used over the last thirty years, but their use has been predominantly practical: they have appeared useful tokens in promoting particular causes, rather than providing possible cues to meaning which required further exploration. Thus, the idea of 'the generic in social work' has been used to promote 'generic' courses of social work training and a common profession of social work. These may or may not be worthy causes, but the terms employed in their promotion have not been used to deepen any sense of curiosity about the nature of social work.

We can now perhaps begin to use the terms 'generic' and 'specific' as explorative tools in education and practice. Yet it is still possible for the tools to become prematurely blunted through the operation of assumptions about a desirable future for the social work profession. For example, in a recent article Studt (1965) dismissed one possible meaning of the term 'fields of social work practice' which equated it with professional specialities or 'institutionalised segments of the profession, sufficiently independent to hamper the development of generalised knowledge and to interfere with the achievement of professional identity.' This is no way to approach a problem of meaning. We cannot elucidate meaning if we have continually to consider the consequences of particular meanings for a cause however worthy. Terms should not be judged on their contribution to professional advancement, but on the way they perform their tasks; and the tasks of words like 'fields of practice', 'generic', 'specific' etc., is to increase our understanding. If a single social work profession does emerge it will be, at least partly, because it has made a contribution to our understanding of the world, including its own operations.

This chapter will begin by indicating the variety of meanings that have been given to the terms 'generic' and 'specific'. No one meaning can easily be canonised, but a review of the different meanings is nonetheless worthwhile. This is partly because some of the basic issues in social work are increasingly discussed in the 'generic-specific' terminology, and partly because the different meanings carry different implications. The terms are not easy to discuss mainly because they are related, so that a meaning given to one affects that given to the other. If, for example, we take 'generic' to mean 'general', then the complementary term would be 'specialised'. Adopting this definition has particular implications. It involves us, for instance, in thinking in terms of the general social worker, on the one hand, and the specialist, on the other. If, however, 'generic' is used in the sense of 'genus' we are lead to think in terms of a common name covering a number of species. In this use of the 'generic-specific' idea a 'generic social worker' as a kind of person like 'the general social worker' mentioned above would not be conceivable; the term 'generic' would refer to those characteristics which make it sensible and convenient to call social workers in different fields by a common name.

A consideration of the meanings of terms cannot, then, be dismissed as 'simply verbal', or as 'merely a matter of semantics'. These reactions, not uncommon amongst social workers, are doubly misleading. Something that was 'simply verbal' would be nonsensical, and particular terms often carry the implications of a way of organising and expressing our experience. This last factor can be well illustrated from the use of the term 'generic', which reinforces the justification for considering its various meanings. As we shall see, a whole way of regarding people and their problems often seems to be contained in the use of the term. This approach—sometimes social workers refer quite simply to their 'generic approach'—has certain characteristics. Man is seen very largely as 'known': he has certain needs which can be listed, and he can be understood mainly in terms of 'common human needs'. 'Generic man', to use a term from Minogue's study of the character of liberal politics (1963), occupies the centre of attention: any particular man, as Minogue suggests, is seen simply as 'generic man' plus certain environmental peculiarities. Similarly, any particular problem is a generic problem plus a simple variation. Thus, such problems as widowhood, the amputation of a limb, and the hospitalisation of a young child, might be described in the terminology under discussion as 'basically about (generic) loss' with certain variations according to whether the loss concerned a spouse, a limb, or a maternal relationship. Lastly, a 'generic approach', as might be expected from its other characteristics, often seems to lead to a particular portrait of the social worker, an expert in human relationships and needs, moving from problem to problem like an eighteenth-century noble, at home everywhere because he is always with the same kind of people.

A marked feature of the use of the terms 'generic' and 'specific' is the failure to distinguish between the different components of social work that we tend to label collectively as 'generic' or 'specific'. It is as if there were a composite 'knowledge-values-skills' that could be described as either generic or specific. More useful results would follow, as was suggested in Chapter 1, if this holistic approach was abandoned and separate questions asked about knowledge, principles or values, and skills. Such questions form the basis of the second section of this chapter.

Finally, this chapter will consider the ways in which the terms 'generic' and 'specific' have been related. As we have already indicated these terms are best seen as complementary, but there are several ways in which terms can be said to complete each other. As we discuss these three aspects of the 'generic-specific' idea—the meaning of the terms, what they refer to (knowledge, values and skills), and the way in which the two terms have been related— it is helpful to bear in mind the key qualifying words that are used, and the concrete nature of social work practice. The qualifying words, such as 'same' or 'similar' ('all social workers use the same knowledge or similar skills') appear eminently clear, but the use of these words in any particular context presupposes agreement about what counts as being the same, and the kinds of resemblance (e.g. family resemblance) intended. Any conclusions about the 'generic-specific' concept must recognise that social work practice at any one time concerns the specific: it is a question of understanding a particular situation confronting a certain client and worker in a particular organisation. This situation cannot be fully understood by discovering the appropriate general theory, if one exists, or effectively handled by recognising the correct covering principle.

Usage of 'generic' and 'specific'

These terms have a longer and more chequered history in America than in Britain. The Milford Conference (1929), for example, stated that 'Generic social case work is the common field to which the specific forms of social case work are merely incidental.' In other passages the conference recorded that 'the outstanding fact is that the problems of social case work and the equipment of the social caseworker are fundamentally the same for all fields', and that 'the trend in training should be towards the development of courses in the methods which are common to all fields of social case work divorced from their specific application in any one field'. These quotations show that American social work was concerned with the terms generic and specific at least thirty years ago but, more significantly, they also show something of the way in which the concern has been expressed. Firstly, the terms are used persuasively, definition (such as it is) and valuation go hand-in-hand: the specific forms of casework are said, for instance, to be *merely* incidental. Secondly, we begin to meet in these quotations some of the key qualifying terms used interchangeably and invariably ever since: words like 'same', 'common', 'fundamental' and, later, 'shared', 'core' and so on. These are not all synonymous terms, but they have been so used, thus hindering the discernment of their different meanings. Thirdly, the quotations demonstrate how easily statements using the two terms move between considerations of practice and of education. It was some time before it was appreciated that arguments in favour of generic social work education did not support any idea of generic social work practice, and that to consider methods divorced from specific application was like looking for the family but ignoring all the members.

Since the Milford Conference the terms have been increasingly used in America, and Bartlett (1959), in a fairly recent discussion of them, has stated that 'At various times "generic" has been taken to mean elementary, non-specialized, common, basic, core, fundamental, essential, comprehensive and whole. Some of the meanings attached to "specific" have been specialized, different, particular and unique.' These terms are clearly different and their difference is greater than that between improvisations on a common theme. 'Elementary' should be complemented by 'advanced', 'unique' seems to stand on its own, 'common' goes with 'special' rather than 'specialised', whilst 'essential' seems to need 'peripheral' as its complement. It is interesting to note that Hollis (1964, p. 214), uses the term 'peripheral' to refer to, amongst other factors, 'the way in which the agency function is defined', though an earlier curriculum report (1948) has stated 'That the major element of difference which is imposed by the special setting is that of agency structure and program' (quoted Bartlett, 1959).

In British social work differences of meaning similar to those found in the longer period of American usage can be found. Yet reference has most frequently been made to 'specialisation' and its complementary. It was, for instance, the specialised nature of the existing separate training programmes for social work which Dame Eileen Younghusband emphasised in the report (1951) which led to the first 'generic' course in Britain. At that time it was probably correct to think of such training as *narrowly* specialised, but it is important to note that there is nothing inevitably narrow about specialisation as such. Helen Bosanquet once observed that a specialist was not a man who knew only one thing, but someone who knew one thing better than other things.

The initial response to the idea of generic training in this country was for *each* field of social work to proclaim or search for that feature of its practice that made it unique. For a while the search was conducted in terms of the difficulties of each field; then in terms of the particular relationships social workers entered into with other disciplines (e.g. the 'unique' aspect of medical social work arose from working contact with doctors). The search for unique features can now be abandoned without losing sight of the importance of the problem of defining as realistically and as accurately as possible the fields of social work. (This will be taken up in the following chapter.) Similarly, we can now admit what should have been obvious from the start that specialisation, which has produced such advances in other fields, is also likely to prove helpful in social work practice. There are, however, several criteria on which such specialisation could be based—knowledge and interest in a particular age group, a certain handicap, or ways of working (e.g. in groups). Each of these has different implications for social work education.

This necessarily brief review of the variety of usage of the terms 'generic' and 'specific' and of some of our past and present attitudes is sufficient to warrant a cautious approach. Yet the next step is not to argue the legitimacy of any one meaning or attitude, but to study the kinds of statements the terms help us to make.

Aspects of practice and education seen as 'generic' and 'specific'

Statements about general aspects of social work education and practice usually refer to the essential equipment of all social workers, sometimes necessary, at other times ideal in terms of knowledge, principles and skills. Thus, in the report mentioned above it was not envisaged that the new 'generic' training programme would

> rule out optional courses for students who know that they intend to become probation officers or almoners or personnel managers or psychiatric social workers or boarding out officers or family case workers, but it does mean that they would study and practise together the common principles and practices which underlie all case work or work with groups of people. They would also consider in common the general causes which underlie both individual and social maladjustment and try to see these in their total social setting rather than concentrating on the delinquent or the neurotic or the deprived or the matrimonially disturbed (Younghusband, 1951).

In this quotation reference is made to common principles and practices underlying social work and to the general causes underlying a range of phenomena. This way of talking raises questions about the relationship between principles and practice, and between the causes and their supposed effects. Do the principles *underlie* the practice or is it more accurate to describe them as constituting it? Are general causes for such a wide range of phenomena as 'individual and social maladjustment' worth searching for, when we have, for instance, abandoned the search for the cause of delinquency as if it were a unitary phenomenon? It may seem that these are unimportant questions, and that nothing very much depends on the distinction, for example, between principles underlying an activity and those that constitute it. This, however, would be a mistaken view. If we are trying to elucidate the nature of social work the question of the description of its principles and their relationship to concrete activity is important. The principles underlying an activity are not as accessible as those that could be described as residing *in* the activity, and the latter provide some criteria for the assessment of good performance. The principles underlying prostitution do not help us to recognise an effective prostitute. Lastly, the distinction between 'in' and 'underneath' is, as we have seen, frequently drawn in social work : we need to exploit every possibility of examining it. The above considerations are examples of the sort of clues that could be neglected when the components of knowledge, of value, and of skill are not separately treated.

Social work knowledge—general

One of the main questions here seems to be what should all social workers know, and what do those in one field of work need that is dispensable for the others?

A good illustration of 'the main body of knowledge which should form part of the common training for all social workers' can be found in the conclusions of Margot Jefferys' survey of the social services in Buckinghamshire

(1965). The quotation is fairly long, but, as has been shown, the subject we are considering requires the close reading of as many detailed statements as possible.

First, the social worker must *have some knowledge* of human growth and development in both its physiological and psychological aspects throughout the chief phases of the life cycle from birth to old age and death. He must *be aware of* the basic human drives and of the significance of the social relationships into which individuals enter especially in their family unit. He must 'know sufficient about health and disease to recognise, and *have some understanding* of, variations within the normal as well as deviations, particularly as manifested in mental and physical handicaps, mental illness, "problem" family living and unmarried parenthood'.

Secondly, all social workers should be *knowledgeable about* the social and economic circumstances in which people live. They must *appreciate* the influence of kin, neighbourhood, school, religion, the work unit and the formal and informal groups in the formation and maintenance of community and group norms and values, and in the attitudes displayed towards those who deviate from these norms.

Thirdly, social work training must give students *a knowledge of* the scope and character of the statutory and voluntary social services. It should deal with forms of social care and the circumstances in which they need to be used. The social worker should *be made aware* of the problems of administering the social care services, of mobilising resources for them, and of determining priorities. In addition, he must become conscious of the need for continuous critical scrutiny of the work of the services. (Italics not original.)

This is in many respects a helpful statement; most of the

aspects mentioned could be taught, at least to some extent. Yet we have to recognise certain problematic features. In the first place this, like every other statement of the knowledge necessary for social work, is based upon expert opinion only. As Karpf (1931, p. 131) remarked much earlier: 'Little if any research has been done, so far as any objective evidence shows, to determine, on a factual basis, what knowledge the social worker requires.' Secondly, we should note the several different modes of awareness indicated in the italicised sections—having a knowledge of, being knowledgeable about, being aware of, appreciating, and so on. Thirdly, it is not easy to know from the above statements what constitutes the necessary and what the sufficient conditions for being called a social worker. Is one not a social worker, for instance, without knowledge of some of the voluntary services, or how much of the kinds of 'knowledge' specified must be possessed before the person is accounted a social worker?

Lastly, we should enquire what counts as human growth, as a phase of life, as a basic human drive, and so on. These appear to be deeply theory-impregnated terms, part of a particular way of regarding our experience. To possess knowledge in these terms is to adopt particular definitions of human behaviour rather than to embark on a consideration of the kinds of definition open to us. Reference to 'basic' drives, like talk of 'common human needs' seems to suggest a kind of 'neutral' human nature which social workers may apprehend, filling in particular variations as they apply their general ideas. Our way, however, of describing human nature is not so much a description of some phenomena existing, as it were 'out there', as a particular way of participating in the world. As Macintyre (1967, p. 268) has observed, in another context, 'The choice of a form of life and the choice of a view of human nature go together.'

Social work knowledge

Earlier reference was made to the knowledge that might be required in one field of work but that was superfluous or peripheral in another. This has not been widely considered in the literature, but a useful treatment of some of the questions involved can be found in Kadushin (1965).

Kadushin identifies different levels of knowledge according to the degree of specificity. Thus, he asks what the following need to know: a worker in a statutory child welfare agency who is conducting a screening interview for a parent considering adoption, a group worker, and all social workers irrespective of field or the method of work they employ. This concrete approach is welcome, even if as we shall see, its actual implementation is open to some question.

In the case of the prospective adopter, Kadushin suggests that the worker should know :

(a) agency rules and their rationale, and she should have achieved some acceptance of them;
(b) the desirable physical conditions of a good adoptive home and a good adoptive neighbourhood;
(c) something about the optimum age differential between adoptive parents and child;
(d) something of the attitudes clients are likely to have regarding the need to come to such an agency and of her own feelings concerning adoption;
(e) she needs to know what feelings she should appropriately convey so as to free the clients to communicate openly. She needs to know how to implement

> these feelings by the appropriate verbal and gestural response to the client's productions. . . . She needs to be able to phrase and intone the questions soliciting such information . . . in a way that will help the clients to answer fully and truthfully. . . . She needs to know how to pace the interview so that it does not start, or end, on too high an emotional level.

This formulation indicates the importance of restraint in conceptualising the things a social worker should know. It seems, at least initially, puzzling to talk in terms of a 'good adoptive *neighbourhood*', and knowledge about the *implementation* of feeling assumes that somehow one 'has' a feeling and then implements it, as one would a plan or idea. Similar difficulties arise when the author discusses 'what every social worker should know', and refers to 'the knowledge and acceptance of the role of social work . . . skill in the application of scientific method . . . in helping the social agency client'. The idea of social work as applied scientific method is not, as will become evident in Chapter 5, immediately clear or convincing, so it is difficult to see how it can be seen as part of essential knowledge.

Social work values

It is often said that social workers share the same values notwithstanding the fact that they practise in markedly different environments. Thus, 'all social work, regardless of the area of specialization is *geared* to the value and needs of the individual.' (Lipeles, 1956, italics not original.) What meaningful proposition is being conveyed in this kind of statement; what difference does it make? The problem is that statements about the value or principles of social work are usually made at such a high level of generality that almost anyone might be said to share them. Unless the values can be discussed at a lower level of generality, it will not be easy to say in what social workers share, and meaningless to adopt the common approach of regarding social work as predominantly the expression of values or the observance of principles.

Some values can be fairly easily understood. Take, for instance, 'confidentiality'. This is discussed as a general principle, and it seems sufficiently straightforward: the client's communications to the social worker are to be treated confidentially. As the principle is applied, however, certain difficulties may arise. How does the social worker deal with the reports he has to make about his client or with knowledge that creates difficulties for him within his organisation (e.g. knowledge of an intended crime or action involving serious risk to others). These kinds of difficulty involve a re-consideration of the principle, since the social worker would wish to establish whether they constitute an exception to a general rule that prescribes confidentiality in usual circumstances or whether the rule itself proscribes the divulging of information except in a number of specified circumstances.

Other values are less easily understood except in relation to a specific circumstance. Take, for instance, the principle of 'acceptance'. Now 'being accepting' is not like 'loving', a word that can be immediately understood, at least to some extent. 'Accepting' seems to contain some hidden reference to that which might prevent something being accepted. Unless this concealed 'in spite of' element is understood 'acceptance' in social work vocabulary would not appear to have much meaning. Thus, a worker's 'acceptance' takes on meaning when, for example, it is realised that he is a child care officer and his client a neglectful or cruel mother: he 'accepts' her, in spite of these qualities.

The subject of social work values is clearly a large one, but in this section it has been treated with the intention of raising two points relevant to the overall consideration of the generic-specific concept. These are the difficulty of appreciating what some of the values mean without considering the general principles in relation to at least a range of concrete circumstances, and the high level of generality at which the subject is usually discussed. Kadushin (1956) has remarked on the gulf between a high level abstraction like 'self-determination' and the social worker sitting in an office with a client, perhaps thinking of himself during or after the interview as putting that principle into practice. Kadushin proposes to fill the gap by means of an empirical enquiry. 'We need to know the specific, repetitive kinds of behaviour engaged in by the worker . . . which are the results of his conscious application of this abstraction.' The argument of this book would not support such a solution on its own. In this field conceptual enquiry is often an essential preliminary, and in this particular instance, we need to give much closer attention to what an abstraction and what applying an abstraction in social work is like before empirical enquiry is likely to be of much help.

Social work skill

We can and do give general descriptions of what social workers do, but there is no general skill so that a worker could become 'qualified in casework as such' (Younghusband, 1951) and then as a medical social worker, child care officer, and so on. Such a conception seems to illustrate the notion already referred to, of social work practice as 'generic' plus certain peculiarities.

There seem to be two main problems in connection with social work skill: what do we mean by it, and how is it acquired? Each of these problems impinge on the generic-specific concept.

Perhaps a social worker could be generally described as someone who invariably attains the objectives of social work. This approach encounters the problem of the relationship between a goal in a particular case (helping Mr. and Mrs. A to treat children less negligently) and such general statements as

> The underlying purpose of all social work effort is to release human power in individuals for personal fulfilment and social good, and to release social power for the creation of the kinds of society, social institutions, and social policy which makes self-realization most possible for all men. (Smalley, 1967, p. 1)

It also faces the difficult issue of formulating the objectives of social work.

Take, for example, the attempt in a recent government report (Ministry of Health, 1959) on social work to use the idea of 'equilibrium' in this connection. The term is used to describe the objectives of social work, but the nature of the balance is doubly unclear. Firstly, the report seems uncertain whether the objective is a 'new' equilibrium or a 'better' one. Secondly, the equilibrium seems to be held in a very wide field indeed. Social work is said to aim at the correction of 'disturbance of equilibrium *in* a given handicapped person and in his family and social relationships.' (Italics not original) Little seems to be added to our stock of information about social work by talking of its aims in this manner.

Perhaps we can say that a skilled social worker is one who 'interviews people well', but how does this achievement distinguish the social worker from the personnel manager? Alternatively, the social worker might be termed 'skilled' if she could apply social work techniques appropriately. Yet, as Woodhouse (1962) has argued, 'Technique cannot be considered without reference to the setting in which it is practised.' Every formulation of general skill will be inadequate without reference to specific tasks in specific agencies, and the reason for this is that the generic concepts of practice are abstract descriptions of what is thought should occur in particular agencies. They are not, as in the case of generic knowledge concepts, explanatory : they cannot be *applied*.

It could, perhaps, be argued that the skills of social work are generic because they are derived from generic knowledge. Thus, Dame Eileen Younghusband states (1964, p. 124), 'The knowledge from this enormous range of subject matter must be very carefully selected and related together as a coherent whole and then some of it translated into social work skill.' Yet the idea of skill or technique as applied science is not without difficulties. According to Oakeshott (1962) a practical activity requires both technical and practical knowledge, and it is only the former that can be formulated in rules. These rules, moreover, have no necessary connection with 'science' or 'theory'. They are descriptions of ways in which particular objectives can be achieved.

The relationship between 'generic' and 'specific'

Some aspects of this have unavoidably been mentioned already, in connection with knowledge, for example. In this section the relationship between 'generic' and 'specific' will be given separate consideration.

Various ways of describing this relationship have been used. Some speak of 'applying the essential elements' or of 'adapting general knowledge and principles' (Hollis, 1964, p. 265), though 'applying' and 'adapting' are clearly different processes, with the second allowing the specific situation to make potentially, at least, much more difference to the general elements. Goldberg (1966) in connection with the knowledge social workers use, speaks of our 'hope to train social workers who share a broad understanding of how different human beings function at different times of their lives in varying social environments. Their specialised knowledge about specific handicaps will be based on this general knowledge of common human needs.' Here, we should enquire into the relationship stated in the phrase 'will be *based* on'. Does this for instance, entail 'exclusively' based? What sort of base will 'a broad understanding' provide? 'Common human needs' is such a slippery concept that it seems unlikely to provide the necessary support. We can envisage a situation in which knowledge of a particular handicap serves as a basis for profitable speculation of a more general kind. For example, a thorough knowledge of deafness may help someone to consider the significance of language for all people living in any particular society.

Concluding questions

This chapter has been concerned with a necessarily brief discussion of some abstract issues, and with raising rather insistently a range of questions concerning matters usually taken for granted. In conclusion, it is suggested that progress in clarifying the issues involved is likely to follow from the attempt to develop curiosity about actual social work experience. If, for instance, one reflects on the experience of moving from one field of social work to another, it is worth asking questions about the move. What was it like? Did it resemble a civil servant changing ministries, a classics master turning to teach German or carpentry, or a lawyer changing from the practice of criminal to the practice of commercial law? As the worker moved, say from child care to probation, what more did he need to know in order to work effectively? Would the situation be adequately described in terms of meeting a familiar set of problems in a different organisational setting or would the worker see himself as confronted with the task of learning the different psychology of those 'seeking help' from the probation service?

4

Casework and its settings

Introduction

In the last chapter we saw that social work was often described as an activity that had generic and specific aspects.
In this chapter we shall examine some of the numerous
statements that describe social work as a range of activities
that take place within a number of specific 'settings'. This
common manner of reference has some connections with
the 'generic-specific' ideas already discussed, but it is also
worth consideration in its own right. The discussion will
take the form of the previous chapter, a consideration of
recent usage, followed by a review of some of the main
ideas we should consider when we think of the settings of
social work. In the previous chapter the emphasis was on
conceptual analysis; in this it will be more on empirical
considerations.

Recent usage

The term 'setting' begins to be widely used in the 1950's
in this country as a response to refined discrimination and
increasing knowledge. As specialisations developed in social

work it began to seem possible to talk about social workers as people pursuing a range of activities, and to see that, to some extent, these activities could be abstracted from the organisations in which they took place. As more became known about such organisations (hospitals, local authorities and so on) a term was required which helped us to look at social work in its various contexts, and to examine the relationship between 'social work' and the organisations in which it was practised. The term 'setting' appeared to meet these requirements. If we compare contemporary views of medical social work with those of the pioneers, who could apparently work satisfactorily with a fairly crude model of social work and little idea of the impact of the hospital on themselves or the patients, we can see some aspects of the development in discrimination and knowledge that required a term like 'settings'.

'Settings' is now a widely used term in this country, but it has not so far been critically considered. The following quotations represent some of the main ways in which it has been recently used.

> *The community care setting* . . . calls for individual action with a change in emphasis. Traditionally the main focus of the work has been with the patient's relatives, and the training has been related to this focus, but most of the community worker's time is spent with the patients themselves. Lastly, it has usually been understood that the *psychiatric social worker's setting* should be found within the therapeutic atmosphere of a hospital or clinic; but the community worker is often part of the administrative structure of a local authority. (Power, 1956)

> One of the most striking features (of an experimental course) was the demonstration we all had that the case-

work approach transcends all differences of setting, each with its policy, functions and limitations. (Smith, 1964)

. . . . the relationship between the psychiatric social worker and the client is central to all psychiatric social work . . . the use of relationships needs to be *carefully* adjusted to the setting in which we work, to the type of client and patient we deal with, and the aims we are pursuing. (Goldberg, 1963) (Italics not original)

Technique cannot be considered without reference to the setting in which it is practised. (Woodhouse, 1962)

The worker, the client, and the setting are the basic components of action and must be viewed as a whole. (Titmuss, 1954)

This last quotation has been widely used: it comes from an article entitled 'The Administrative Setting of the Social Services'.

Finally, the term is used more widely, when, for instance we refer to the 'welfare setting' (Goldberg, 1966) or 'the individual in his social setting'. In these instances the framework of social work or of individual activity is so widened that it is difficult to see what constraints or influences are intended.

In the examples given both differences and family resemblances can be found. The setting can be the individual worker's, something like a framework he carries around with him, and within which he conducts his social work in whatever style he pleases. Or setting is the name of the organisation in which the social worker works, or the name of a programme which his agency is helping to carry out (e.g. the community care setting in mental health). Alternatively, the reference is more concrete and more general: the courts, the hospitals, and so on are seen as providing a 'setting' for social work or the social worker.

47

Finally, we may abstract a particular organisational feature as dominant, at least from the point of view of social work. Thus, in psychiatric social work frequent reference is made to 'the clinical setting', and in probation to an 'authoritarian' one.

Each of these different ways of using the term has some disadvantages. The last, for instance, often prevents us seeing what actually occurs in 'the settings' already judged to be 'clinical', or 'authoritarian', and the designation of some 'setting' as typically or uniquely clinical or authoritarian may support a false classification. Thus, the mental hospital and the child guidance clinic have both been seen as 'clinical settings', but, as Hollis (1956) has suggested, some child guidance clinics resemble some family casework agencies more than mental hospitals. Similarly, the agreement at one time common amongst social workers that the probation service provided the typical instance of social work in an authoritarian setting prevented social workers from examining the ways in which authority might be said to operate in other services. In a sense, legal authority monopolised the social worker's view of authority, and for a period there was little or no recognition of different kinds of authority.

The examples also indicate different valuations given to 'settings'. For some it is the limitations that are stressed: the setting is perhaps something which frustrates the worker and from which he would like to escape if only he knew how. Others see the 'setting' as valuable in terms of actual work with clients. Their argument in graphical terms would be that the setting gets into the relationship between client and worker as a central factor that cannot be avoided and can be constructive. The setting is part of the action. In saying this, however, we introduce a distinction of importance. Titmuss, in the above quotation, refers to 'three necessary components of *action*', but does not sufficiently distinguish between the different purposes of 'viewing the action as a whole'. Do we wish to view the action as a whole in order to understand it fully or in order to act appropriately? In other words, are we speaking an observer language or an agent language? This distinction is often simply overlooked. For example, in a recent book casework is seen 'as an administrative process as well as a treatment process' (agent language), but the author also argues that 'one cannot understand what social caseworkers actually do in various situations unless one sees their work with their clients in the context of other relationships with administrators, colleagues, committee members, and members of the public individually and collectively'. (observer language) (Forder, 1966, p. 11 and p. 199). There is no limit that we can place on our efforts to understand what social workers do, and we glimpse this as we see the ever widening circles that the author mentions; surely 'members of the public collectively' is simply another way of referring to 'society'? The agent, however, has to act before his society is understood and he should act within the best possible perspective. What should constitute this perspective? Where can we draw the boundaries of his understanding short of the universe?

Criticisms of the term and alternatives

The term 'setting' has perhaps some lingering undertones from its use in other circumstances. We refer to the setting of a play or a jewel. The action of the play takes place in a more or less fixed setting, and a jewel is held in a permanent relationship to its setting by its setting. It is this

49

aspect of the term that has been criticised in recent American work; the idea, that is, of a permanent, unchanging framework for action or existence, a space in which to practise. Thus Studt (1965) has argued that the term 'setting' evoked a constricting and passive image of the relationships between the social worker and his environment. 'It located the practitioner in an organisational box to which he had to "adjust" but for which he was not responsible. In this perspective, everything outside the "real" work done by the social worker with his client could be conceived as a bureaucratic "frame" subtly limiting or distorting the practice of social work method.'

Similarly Bartlett (1961) has complained that 'setting' focuses too much attention on administrative aspects and on working relationships within the agency and gives insufficient attention to the reasons for the agency's existence and to the body of knowledge, values and methods on which the agency's services rest.

Clearly these shortcomings cannot reside, as it were, in the term. They are connected with our usage of the term, but they are serious shortcomings and we should certainly consider the use of a new term. American social work seems to favour 'field of practice'. This has been most clearly developed by Bartlett (1961) and, since it amounts to a fresh way of looking at social work as a whole, it is worth some attention.

Bartlett's ideas can be summarised in terms of three propositions which help us to describe social work practice, to discern the main characteristics of a field, and to prescribe the conditions that must obtain in any field before social work can be practised within its boundaries. Firstly, social work practice is seen as a 'constellation of value, purpose, sanction, knowledge and method', and all the elements must be present to some degree. Secondly, 'a field' has four main characteristics, a problem of central concern; a system of organised services; knowledge, value and methods; and it is influenced by and composed of certain sociocultural attitudes. Thus, in the field of health the problem of central concern is health and disease from an individual and social viewpoint; the system of organised services are the various services for physical (and mental?) health; the knowledge, value and methods are those of medicine, and the sociocultural attitudes concern all sick people generally and those with specific diseases. Thirdly, the mingling of social work practice and the characteristics of any one field constitute social work practice in that particular field. Yet a field must also allow social work practice its own identity. In the health field, for instance, the psychosocial aspects of illness must be recognised. Social workers cannot function appropriately as facilitators helping the wheels of an organisation to turn or supplementing the activities of other professions.

The idea of a field of practice has been consistently developed by Bartlett, and has gained wide acceptance in America. How should social workers appraise it, deciding to adopt or reject it in this country? This kind of issue, rarely debated in social work, is crucial to the present book, which is arguing amongst other things that more is at stake in proposals for a change in terminology than in suggestions that a woman would improve her appearance by changing her dress. We have to ask what does the concept of 'field of practice' help us to attend to that is ignored in the idea of 'setting'; what does it enable us to say more precisely? An examination of the concept from this perspective enables us to make a number of critical points.

Firstly, Bartlett's arguments, (as summarised above) constitute a kind of 'package deal', in the course of which a number of claims on behalf of social work are almost taken for granted. For example, the existence of a distinctive 'constellation' of social work values, purposes, sanctions, knowledge and method. We have already seen in Chapter 2 some of the difficulties that arguments along these lines have to face. This is not, of course, to suggest, let alone say, that such difficulties *cannot* be met, only to make the necessary point that they have not been met so far. Again, Bartlett's argument has to assume, because it is also advancing professional claims, that there is something derogatory in helping the machinery of an organisation to work. Many social workers in the past have seen this as an important part of their work, and their activities could also be described as supplementary to those of other professions. On what grounds can we justify a condemnation of their approach?

Secondly, the arguments combine description and prescription in ways that are not always apparent. This, as we have seen, is a feature of social work arguments in general. Take, for example, the idea of a 'problem of central concern'. This seems to describe 'what a field has been established to achieve', but the objectives of a field are likely to be numerous, and we require a criterion to enable us to judge between them. The idea of a 'problem of central concern' is like that of 'primary task', also used in the analysis of organisations. Both are legitimising concepts based on a consensus rather than a conflict view of society. People may well be in conflict over the identity of the problem of central concern, though it may be difficult to see this when such problems are stated in such broad terms as 'health'. When they are in conflict, say, over the problem of central concern in the penal field, it is not easy to see how their arguments could be settled.

On the other hand—and this is the third point to be made—Bartlett's analysis does enlarge our view of the environment in which social workers operate. This probably represents a gain on the concept of 'setting'. Reference to a field of practice helps us to view a wider range of influences more easily, without removing the boundaries altogether. It gives a social worker something in which to specialise, and does justice to the complexity of the work. A social worker is seen within a field of influences rather than established in a particular administrative framework. This is in keeping with recent developments in thinking about social administration in this country. The reiterated theme of a recent text (Donnison, 1965) in this subject is simply that 'organisations' do not, as it were lie around waiting to be studied.

Crucial aspects

Whatever the term used, what essential aspects of social work should we be helped to portray? There are at least two main aspects. Social workers and clients always meet and work in an organisation within which they play different roles. The organisation largely defines the work they do and profoundly influences both client and social worker. These two aspects will now be treated in more detail.

Workers and clients within the organisation

When we talk of 'setting' or field of practice, we nearly

always refer to the worker. Thus, when Hollis (1956) suggests that the social history differs very little between agencies, she is thinking primarily from the worker's point of view. We should, however, recognise that the client has always to assume a role within the organisation, and that this role is probably different at the three main stages of beginning, maintenance and ending. We can see, for example, that in some fields the client is often asked initially to assume the role of informant. He may later become, in some instances, something like a co-worker. So, once we begin to think in terms of the client's role *vis-à-vis* the organisation of which he becomes a member we also begin to consider changes in role in the typical client's career. If, moreover, we take seriously the idea of membership we find ourselves asking questions concerning the terms on which membership is granted. Does the client's organisational role carry social degradation? How far does this role affect the client's status in other roles? For instance, Mayer and Rosenblatt (1964) have suggested that clients may prematurely end contact with a welfare agency not because of a defect in the worker-client relationship but because of reactions in his circle of intimates to his client status.

Understanding organisations may seem an overwhelming task. Take the example of the hospital. In a recent review of the literature on hospitals Perrow (1965) listed 128 references, saying that probably half as many again were examined but not mentioned, and half as many again were not even examined. We are, moreover, only at the beginning of understanding the three main factors that influence organisations: the cultural system that sets legitimate goals, the technology that determines the means available for reaching them, and the social structure of the organisation in which specific techniques are embedded. However, all this would be overwhelming only if we thought we had to make every social worker into a sociologist of organisations. Our task is more limited but no less important and we have to begin with a number of simple axioms. These would include, take current professional terminology with a pinch of salt.

For example, there is considerable emphasis at present on the professional idea of 'the team'. This is used with such apparent compulsion that the typical social worker may be defined as one who says 'Where two or three are gathered together, there is a team.' The insistent use of this concept of 'the team' may in fact be dysfunctional. It may represent an ideal (perhaps of professional advancement as much as anything) but its frequent unreflective use prevents us seeing the reality. It prevents us seeing the interdisciplinary conflicts that frequently occur, and leads us to assume that the fully-staffed 'team' is a pervasive phenomenon. Yet in the field of child psychiatry, for instance, in 1963, only 57 of the 146 local education authorities had a complete child guidance 'team', and of these, only 2 were in the Northern Region and 4 in Wales.

Now this information is not readily available: it has to be extracted from Ministry returns. And this raises a point of considerable importance. How do we learn about settings or fields so that we can do more than perpetuate myths and ideals? Does it matter, for example, that it is extremely difficult to make any substantiated general statement about the child guidance service? Yet if we can make no generalisations about clinics, hospitals etc., it is difficult to see how we can continue to talk of 'settings' or 'fields of practice' in a helpful way.

The significance of the organisation

We are only beginning to investigate this, and much of what is taught in connection with either clients or workers is speculative. In the following discussion reference will be made only to the social worker's position.

It seems possible to begin to generalise about the attitudes social workers may take to their agency. Thus, in a recent study of 110 American caseworkers Billingsley (1964) posed a number of questions concerning what a social worker should do in certain conflict situations.

The responses to the six conflict situations are of interest. Only a quarter were in favour of meeting the client's needs even if this required violating explicit agency policy : 57 per cent if this meant violating stated professional standards and 95 per cent if violating the expectation of the community; 61 per cent of the workers were in favour of carrying out agency policy even if this required violating stated professional standards and 97 per cent if it meant violating community expectation. 98 per cent were in favour of action according to professional standards even if this meant violating community expectation. The author concluded that social workers in fact adopted a number of general orientations. There were 'the professionals', primarily oriented to the profession 'outside' the agency; the bureaucrats who gave primacy to agency policy; 'the conformists' adopting both a professional and a bureaucratic orientation; and, finally, 'the innovators' who showed a fairly low commitment to both agency policies and professional standards.

This kind of empirical investigation is of importance in suggesting the variety of response a social worker may make to the organisation in which he works. It also raises questions of theoretical significance. If, for example, 95 per cent of the workers were in favour of meeting the client's needs even if this involved violating community expectation, should we not reconsider the view, referred to in Chapter 2, of social work as 'society's conscience'?

Yet investigation along such lines does not exhaust the question of the significance of the agency for the worker. Some would argue that particular workers are motivated to work in one field rather than another because of the emotional significance of the problems typically presented in and by that field. Thus, it would be argued that a person who needed to come to terms with his delinquent tendencies would be attracted to probation. This approach is sometimes taken further, and it is suggested that the structure of the agency enables a social worker both to begin a contact with a particular problem, and also to maintain some necessary distance from it. This appears to be a plausible hypothesis, which helps to explain, amongst other things, the comparatively small degree of mobility between fields of work. We can only judge its plausibility in terms of our own experience, until the hypothesis is crucially tested. However, it illuminates one of the important areas to which a concept like 'setting' or 'field of work' should direct our attention.

5

Social work as science or art

The two preceding chapters have dealt with topics that could be termed 'domestic' from the point of view of social work. In this and the following chapter the frame of reference will be wider. Social work has often been called a science or an art, and various attempts have been made to distinguish social work from friendship and from analytical therapy. We may not easily be able to grasp the generic and specific aspects of social work or see the significance of settings: we all have some kind of a concept of science, art and friendship. The form of this chapter follows that of the two previous chapters, an attempt to discern the different ways in which social work and science or art have been linked, followed by a discussion of the main issues.

Social work and science

This is obviously a topic of very wide dimensions, and it will be considered at greater length in another volume in this series. The focus of this chapter will be on those aspects of the relationship between social work and science relevant to the present theme.

'Science' is a concept that can be used in a number of different ways, and it has also high positive and negative value for social workers. It can dazzle or dismay the practitioner, and it has had a place in social work language since the second half of the nineteenth century. Toynbee, at the beginning of the movement leading to present day social work, claimed that we should aim at making existing benevolence scientific. Since then science has been linked with social work in many different ways, some of which have involved reference to 'art' seen as the negative or complementary to 'science'. C. S. Loch (1899) argued that charity 'is not spasmodic, casual and emotional, but, like science, an all-observing, all-comprising intelligence. It is not antagonistic to science: it is science—the science of life—in operation—knowledge doing its perfect work.' Karpf (1931) in one of the few attempts at an empirical investigation of the knowledge social workers actually use quotes with approval (p. 86) Lowie's statement that 'as the engineer calls on the physicist for a knowledge of mechanical laws . . . so the social builder of the future who would seek to refashion the culture of his time and add to its cultural values, will seek guidance from ethnology, the science of culture, which in Taylor's judgement is "essentially a reformer's science".'

Halbert (1923, p. 25) saw the social worker ideally as 'a person with thorough knowledge of the social sciences who is skilled in the specialised business of the influencing of, by scientific methods, individuals who constitute society, the organisations or institutions that enter into the constitution of society . . . so as to cause them to function in accordance with human welfare with greater efficiency.'

More recently Keith-Lucas (1966) has written of 'The Art and Science of Helping', while Leonard (1966) has argued that the social work teacher should 'help students to understand the nature of scientific explanation in order that they may be better able to evaluate and use the results of the social sciences in social work practice'. Other writers have seen the social worker as a 'behavioural technologist' (Jehu, 1966, p. 117), or have referred to 'scientific assumptions' in social work: for example, 'human behaviour is governed by psychological or social laws rather than being erratic and accidental' (Hollis, 1955). Social work methods have been said to resemble scientific method, and Reynolds (1964) has referred to social casework as 'a valid concept of scientific social adjustment'. Finally, Bisno (1952) lists as one of the assumptions of social work, that human behaviour can be studied because it is determined.

These references, representing only a few of the viewpoints that have been expressed, imply a wholehearted welcome for 'science'. It is not easy to find examples of a contrary position. This is partly because such a position is often viewed as essentially a moral one, which can be stated only with difficulty and argued not at all. The point of view which questions the high value given to 'science' in social work finds expression more often than not in conversation rather than in social work literature. Thus, the concern is voiced that the emphasis on 'science' will turn the warm-hearted social servant into a cold clinician manipulating people and more interested in creating a laboratory than conducting a home visit. Alternatively, the 'scientific' social worker is seen as someone who wishes to reduce the area of human choice or to deny the influence of one human person on another. Such points of view are not usually seen as parts of an argument, either by those who adopt them or by those who criticise. In so far as argument is envisaged it is seen in the form, social work is an art, not a science. This position will be considered later. The point to be made here is that the positive statements illustrated in the preceding two paragraphs can be systematically discussed: the only responses are not a simple acceptance or denial. This is so, however, only if we recognise the wider universe of discourse which provides their context. A consideration of this context, of what 'being scientific' can mean, shows amongst other things, that what we sometimes see as 'the essence' of science, may only be a relatively unimportant trimming.

A good example of distinguishing, appropriate criteria for judging investigations to be 'scientific' can be found in Miles (1966). He lists the following commonly accepted criteria: an investigation is scientific if it takes place in a laboratory, controls the experimental conditions, is repeatable, and if its results are recorded by a reliable observer, and are such that any observer in a similar position would report them in the same way. Science, moreover, is commonly considered to be concerned not with particular occurrences but with framing general laws; findings are not scientific unless expressed in quantitative terms; if a particular explanation is put forward, it must be possible by means of experiments to exclude other possibilities. Finally, scientific concepts must be defined operationally, i.e. be described without superfluous theoretical superstructure, and we must always be ready to say what would constitute definitive grounds for the truth of what we say. Miles argues that the first and second criteria are only part of the trappings of scientific respectability and that the repeatability criterion would exclude a number of reputable studies, including cosmology and parts of astronomy. It is possible also to argue that some of the other criteria may not be as crucial as suggested, but the important points in the present argument are that we should be clear about the criteria we adopt, and that we should beware of the danger of envisaging the attempt to be 'scientific' as a question of the slavish observance of pre-ordained rules.

The usage of 'science'

In the previous section a number of quotations showed how persistently social work and science have been linked. They also demonstrate the different ways in which the relationship has been envisaged. In this section two main ideas of the connection between science and social work have been selected for discussion: the first, illustrated in the above quotation from Loch, is the apparently trivial view that 'science' is the equivalent of unemotional, clear thinking; the second sees social work either as a science in its own right or—and this is now the more common view —as an applied science.

For some writers, then, 'being scientific' in social work means thinking clearly and systematically in ways uninfluenced by the emotions. This is obviously an unhelpful way to consider the question, but reflection on why it is unhelpful leads to two important points. The first is that many different kinds of statement can be clear and form part of a systematic argument: poetic statements, historical and philosophical statements can all be clear in their different ways, but this, of course, does not make them 'scientific'. There are many ways of being intelligible. There are, for instance, no unambiguously 'scientific' referrants in the general statement that 'Professional practice proceeds from a set of clear principles and concepts about human beings and their needs which are consciously held, teachable as such, and which constitute the logical justification for the practice.' Nor can they be found in such particular principles as 'man is knowable', or 'phenomena are understandable contextually'. Yet both the general statements and the principles are placed under the heading 'Scientific Base' in *A Conceptual Framework for Social Casework* (Cockerill *et al.*, 1952).

Secondly, the idea of 'science' as essentially unemotional provides a good example of the acceptance of an unreal notion of 'science' mentioned earlier. Emotions play an important part in scientific discovery, not simply in the elation that often accompanies discovery, but also in scientific work itself. Polanyi (1958), for example, argues 'that scientific passions are no mere psychological by-product, but have a logical function which contributes an indispensable element to science. They respond to an essential quality in a scientific statement and may accordingly be said to be right or wrong, depending on whether we acknowledge or deny the presence of the quality in it.' If this line of argument is accepted, there is no necessity to attempt to distort social work (by trying to make it 'unemotional') in order to meet supposed canons of scientific respectability.

Yet the urge in social work to meet some kind of criteria of scientific respectability seems insistent: claims that social work is already a science, is beginning to constitute a science, or is an applied science, have been made successively since the middle of the last century. What is involved in such claims? To answer this question it is helpful to treat separately the two main assertions: social work is a science and social work is best seen as an applied science.

Social work is a science

When scientific status is claimed for social work, three considerations seem to be involved: the social worker knows the laws governing human behaviour and simply applies them; social work methods resemble scientific method; social work is a technical matter. Each of these three ways of interpreting the claim that social work is a science will now be considered.

At first glance it may appear that the view of a social worker as applying the laws of human behaviour is the same as that which sees social work as an applied science. Yet there is an important difference. Take, for example, Loch's statement (1899): 'Put it as we may, life, the good life, is a hard struggle for everyone, to whatever class he may belong. As the wicked make haste to be rich, so the philanthropists make haste to reform. And life rebukes both. It says: Science has laws which you cannot surpass, though you may understand and work co-operatively with them.' Concerning the subject of eugenics, he wrote (1904): '. . . unless definite laws are discovered which can be practically turned into social commandments and can be stated and preached with a kind of religious fervour it seems hardly possible to make very much further progress on such a question.' In a similar vein Thomas observed (1909, pp. 10-11): 'It is no exaggeration to say that a social worker without some knowledge of the laws of social welfare . . . might be likened to a man who, without a scientific knowledge of physical and mechanical laws and forces, should attempt to construct a mountain railway.'

In these quotations, particularly in those from Loch, we can see clearly expressed the notion that the appropriate attitude towards scientific laws was one of obedience. In this context the social worker acted as an administrator of the laws that were assumed to govern human behaviour. When we come to consider the view that social work is an applied science it will be evident that such an approach allows, as it were, more freedom of activity on the part of the person applying the law and acknowledges the difference the situation might make to any particular application of a law. Loch, and those who thought like him, conceived of scientific laws dictating what social workers, amongst others, should do. Yet, as another social work teacher of the time later pointed out, science might be considered as dictating to a man who wished to build a bridge, but 'for the society which wants to reach a better social state there is no such science.' 'In social life there are no definite, limited, clearly definable ends, for all ends or aims, even those which seem most obvious and certain, are relative to the indefinable and ever-changing general ideals by which we are animated.' (Urwick, 1912)

The claim that social work is a science, made in its strong form by the pioneers of modern social work, was based not so much on a distorted picture of social work practice in their time, but rather on a misleading view of the jurisdiction of 'science'. The claim would probably not be made today in its strong form, though it lingers perhaps in the way certain theories—notably of a psycho-analytic kind—are used by some social workers. What is much more common is the weaker form of the claim, namely that social work method resembles or should resemble scientific method.

Two examples of this kind of claim will be considered: Lehrman (1954) and Eaton (1959).

Lehrman wishes to establish the existence of a 'diagnostic mode of reasoning' which helps the social worker to progress through what he describes as 'the sequential steps in the diagnostic scientific method'. This diagnostic reasoning is of the following kind:

Mr. Jones is irresponsible
Psychopaths are irresponsible
Therefore there is a probability that Mr. Jones is a psychopath.
Mr. Jones is impulsive
Psychopaths are impulsive
Therefore there is a great probability that Mr. Jones is a psychopath.

Now, it is clearly important to describe the steps social workers take in reaching judgements about people and categorising them, but reference to ways in which categorisation is attempted in, say, biological science suggests ways in which Lehrman's attempt might be appraised. Grene (1961) for example, in a recent discussion of the logic of biology, draws attention to Pantin's paper on 'The Recognition of Species'. Pantin contrasts the yes-no matching of specimens by museum taxonomists with what he describes as the informal 'aesthetic' recognition of species in the field. He suggests that what he is comparing is a deductive process (such as Lehrman outlines) with the intuitive recognition of an individual as belonging to a certain classification, a being of a certain kind. It is this intuitive recognition that enables his students not to return empty-handed when he instructs them to collect 'all the worms that sneer at you'. Grene considers that Pantin's intuitive element is the equivalent of Polanyi's unspecifiable components of knowledge—i.e. those constituents of knowledge which cannot be stated in the form of propositions or arguments even though they are indispensable to it. This is clearly part of a large and complex argument, the detailed exposition of which is inappropriate in the present book. Two comments are, however, appropriate. Firstly, even in such an apparently simple exercise as classification, it is impossible to describe completely the operations that occur. Secondly, in claiming that social work methods resemble those of science, it is important to observe that there may be differences between sciences in respect of method. Grene has argued that what she describes as the recognition of pattern and relevance can be discarded in the exact sciences, but that in biology it always plays an important part. And this is because it *is* biology and not, as some would claim, only on its way to being physics and chemistry.

Eaton's discussion of a scientific basis for social work takes the form of an exposition of similarities between research and practice in terms of the definition, analysis and resolution of problems. The following are examples from each of these categories.

Problem Definition

Practice	*Research*
Choice of problem to be acted on in a specific case.	Choice of problem to be studied generally.

Problem Analysis

Accumulation of relevant evidence by scientific methods.	Accumulation of relevant evidence by scientific methods.
Diagnosis: formulation of an explanation of the evidence.	Analysis: formulation of an explanation of the evidence.

Problem Resolution

Treatment: action to deal with the problem on the basis of the diagnosis.	*Prediction:* projection of the analysis on a new situation to test its validity.

Eaton represents a detailed account of the processes of social work practice and of research, but is his description of practice and of research accurate? An idealised version of both or either would sterilise the argument. Consequently, we should address our questions to the practice of social work and the practice of research. When, for instance, Eaton suggests that both kinds of practitioner have to choose a problem, does the apparent similarity of the situation conceal the different factors that must influence the form of their decision. Thus, when Bowlby (1958) talks of the reasons for his choice of child separation as a subject for research, he suggests only partly the *kinds* of reasons that might lead a social worker to concentrate on a particular problem in a family. He says:

> Firstly, results have an immediate and valuable application; secondly, it is an area in which we can get comparatively firm data and so show those still hyper-critical of psychoanalysis that it has good claims to scientific status; finally, the experience of young child being separated from his mother provides us with a dramatic if tragic example of psycho-pathology—the generation of conflict so great that the normal means of its regulation are shattered.

This description of the different reasons for choosing a particular field of research bears some relation to the reasons for choosing a problem for solution in social work practice, but it seems to neglect, for example, the complex bargaining process in which social worker and client participate before some mutual agreement is reached on the problem to be worked at.

Similarly, both practitioner and research worker look for evidence, but the social worker is not necessarily searching for scientific evidence. There are different kinds of statement (historical, aesthetic, legal and so on), and each of them would be supported by different kinds of evidence. Thus, Mary Richmond's (1917) important work *Social Diagnosis* is concerned at least as much with a legal kind of evidence as with the kind that might help to constitute a scientific proof.

Lastly in this section we must consider that interpretation of social work as science which emphasises the technical aspects of social work. Keith-Lucas (1966) in the article already referred to says ' "Social work" is a science —there are principles, even, though I don't like the word, "techniques".' Yet we should enquire how far 'science' and 'technology' are synonymous. Polanyi (1951) contrasts the ways in which the two develop. The science of mechanics, for instance, has developed over the last four centuries on the same basic ideas; each new phase re-stating what was known before and revealing that its predecessor was the embryo of a truth wider and deeper than itself. Technology progresses differently: each new step represents a new departure, each new form simply replaces its predecessor. The scientist can work successfully only in a community which is responsive and critical, imbued with devotion to a subject. An inventor, on the other hand, does not have to immerse himself entirely in one branch of scientific knowledge. He must remain aware of a certain set of practical circumstances.

In this section we have been concerned with various meanings given to the idea that social work is a science. We have seen that at one stage of social work history the practitioner was seen as the servant of the scientific laws that governed human behaviour. More recently writers have remarked on the resemblances between the methods of science and social work. Others see the claim for scientific status resting on the technical aspects of social work. None of these ideas can be pursued to a firm conclusion in the present work. The aim of this section has been rather to indicate possible next steps in arguments that would consider the validity of these ideas.

Social work as applied science

This formulation of the relationship between social work and science has gained in popularity in recent years. There are writers concerned with the theoretical analysis of social work who question the assumed distinction between pure and applied science (Greenwood, 1955). Whilst others see the formulation as entirely a programme for future achievement. Pollak (1951), for instance, states that 'the history of the relation between social science and social welfare practice, by and large, has been one of estrangement and separation.' Both viewpoints merit further exploration, but for the purposes of this section we must assume the distinction implied, and that the formulation of social work as an applied science expresses something more than a wish for the future. Three aspects of this formulation have been selected for discussion, but they by no means exhaust the subject. Is social work simply an applied science? Is there only one way of conceiving an applied science? Can other professions be viewed in this way, and, if so, can any lessons be deduced for social work?

In asking the first question—is social work simply an applied science—it is helpful to examine other fields in which questions of applying a complex body of knowledge arise. Such a procedure is in fact an essential element in the approach adopted in this book. Take, for example, the issue Devons (1961) has raised in the field of economics: 'Applied Economics—the Application of What?'. He quotes with approval an observation by Keynes: 'The Theory of Economics does not furnish a body of settled conclusions immediately applicable to policy. It is a method rather than a doctrine, an apparatus of mind, a technique of thinking, which *helps* its possessor to draw correct conclusions.' (Italics not original) Devon argues that the application of economics depends very heavily on a few selected propositions; it is, he says, the most elementary propositions that matter; for example, such commonsense axioms about the economic facts of life as 'bygones are bygones', 'you cannot have your cake and eat it'. His warning that 'it is so easy and dangerous to mistake description and classification of situations in a special economic language as answers to problems' could profitably be applied to those who place undue reliance on the capacity of either sociological or psychological theories to solve the problems encountered in social work. Devons concludes by stating that 'In any case a theoretical model cannot be based on mere introspection and thought about logical relations. It must have some relation to reality, and the appropriate elements of reality to assume can only be selected by some process other than that of model building.' His discussion of some of the issues raised by the idea of applied economics has clear relevance for the question whether social work is simply an applied science.

Some of the issues are raised in a discussion (Gouldner, 1956) which argues that there can be more than one way of conceiving an applied social science. Gouldner adopts something of Devons' position when he states that 'The applied social sciences cannot be fruitfully regarded as springing Athena-like from the furrowed brow of the pure disciplines. Any metaphor which conceives of applied social science as the offspring, and of the basic disciplines as parents, is misleading.' He suggests that the applied social scientist uses the concepts rather than the generalised propositions of social science, and that he must be 'prepared to make his own theoretical innovations'. Finally, he offers two possible models for the applied social scientist, an engineering model and a clinical model. The former involves accepting the problem to be solved as defined by the client (usually an organisation), consulting only with those who have hired the research worker, and claiming to be 'value-free'. The second model involves 'diagnosing' the problem presented, consulting with all groups concerned, and not claiming to be 'value-free'. If Gouldner's argument is correct, it is clearly insufficient to describe the social worker as an applied scientist. One has to enquire which kind of applied scientist he most closely resembles.

In thinking about science and social work it is important to consider the relationship between scientific enquiry, professional practice and also some kind of practice theory, which, as Greenwood (1956) has suggested, aims at the control rather than the explanation of phenomena. The last question in this section concerns the experience of other professional groups in considering this relationship. Obviously it would be useful to reflect on a wide range of professions, but for present purposes it will be sufficient to reflect on one profession, that of nursing. Wald and

Leonard (1966) have examined the development of a practice theory for nursing, and their description and conclusions seem to have interesting parallels with social work. They state that all previous attempts to develop a scientific body of knowledge basic to nursing practice have tried to apply 'the basic sciences' to nursing practice. Nurses have looked for a scientific underpinning of their practice to medicine, to education and to industrial management, and now the social sciences are being combed for basic concepts which could be integrated into the nursing curriculum. Wald and Leonard argue that the 'basic sciences' may not provide the best or even a ready source of support for practice. It is preferable to begin with nursing practice and to develop concepts from the analysis of clinical experience rather than to try to make borrowed concepts fit the practice.

Social work as art

'While the principles upon which charity should be given form a science, the actual administration of charity to a poor person is an art of very great importance.' (Report of Annual Meeting of C.O.S., 1894.) This presentation of social work as both an art and a science represents a common position, but in the 1910's and 1920's in America it was not unusual to find definitions which interpreted social casework exclusively as an art. Indeed, approximately a third of the definitions given in Swithun Bowers' study (1949) refer to casework as an art. For example, Richmond defines casework as 'the art of doing different things for and with different people by co-operating with them to achieve at one and the same time their own and society's betterment' (quoted Bowers), whilst Moore calls casework 'an art, our effort to interpret and preserve the aesthetic values in human relationships' (quoted Bowers). This is in fact one of the few statements that accepts the term 'art' in its full meaning, appreciating that 'art' involves at least some reference to aesthetics. Most other definitions refer to art in the weaker sense of 'skill'. They intend perhaps to call attention to the non-routine aspects of social work rather than to encourage us to think of the caseworker's creativity and originality as an artist, or to claim that the caseworker resembles the artist who is, in Richards' judgement (1924), more capable than the non-artist of organising his own responses.

The more usual claim that social work is both an art and science involves a number of considerations. It leads us to consider what counts as an art or a science, which aspects of social work can profitably be described as art and which as science, and, finally, how 'art' and 'science' are related in social work. In this section special attention will be given to the division between knowledge or principles and skill to be found in the quotation at the beginning of the section.

We have already seen that references to social work as 'art' usually mean social work as skill. Only the Functional School of social work in America (to be discussed in the following chapter) pays much attention to the idea of 'form' (Smalley, 1967). Now the examination of what we mean by a skilful performance, by an ability, and so on has been an object of philosophical enquiry from the time of Aristotle. It has assumed recent importance in the work of such philosophers as Ryle (1967) and Oakeshott (1967). Oakeshott's work in particular can be used as a basis for a discussion of the separation often made in social work between knowledge and skill. Its use in this way illustrates again the importance of considering the problems that arise

74

in social work in the light of wider issues and with the aid of other disciplines.

Oakeshott argues that all we can be said to know constitutes a manifold of different abilities. What we are aware of is not a number of items of knowledge available for use, but the possession of power of specific kinds— to solve a legal problem, to perform an operation, and so on. These abilities are a compound of information and judgement. All knowledge contains an ingredient of information which may range from what Oakeshott calls 'the recognitions and identifications' in which knowledge of any sort emerges from indeterminate awareness, to rules which inform the skills in which we carry what we may be said to know. This information, however, never constitutes the whole of what we know. Before any concrete ability can appear information must be patterned by judgement which is an implicit component of knowledge unspecifiable in propositions.

This approach to knowledge as skill sheds light on a number of problems in social work. It helps, for example, to make meaningful the frequent references to social work students 'taking in' and 'making their own' certain aspects of social work knowledge. In the terminology of the above paragraph these would now be considered students who had become able to use particular abilities: reference to an internal world furnished with pieces of information would be unnecessary. Again, it helps to resolve some of the problems hitherto expressed in terms of 'intuition' and 'theoretical knowledge'.

6

The social worker as friend or therapist

Social work as friendship

The more perceptive nineteenth-century social worker saw her task as the repair of relationships broken by the social changes consequent on the first Industrial Revolution. Before those changes, social work was an ingredient of other tasks: as Octavia Hill (1893) expressed it, 'district visiting was less *work* than neighbourly kindness taking its natural course in the flow of help to individuals who had long been known'. In her re-socialising task, however, the social worker was faced with the problem of identifying her role. Sometimes, the simple re-creation of rural arcadia and the social relations appropriate to it seemed a sufficient objective and model. At other times the master-servant relationship appeared helpful. What was required was a term for transactions between social workers and those they were trying to help which did justice to the emerging character of those transactions. This character seems to consist of two main elements: the central part played by the social worker's own personality, and the importance of reciprocity.

The early social workers did not talk of 'using' their personalities or their relationships with their clients, but they recognised the importance of the social worker's personality. 'Social work,' wrote Bernard Bosanquet (1901), 'is thought of as something spontaneous, human, sociable; an effort to gain direct contact with the human nature of those around us. In it we devote to others, not our peculiar acquired skill, but ourselves, our heart and soul.' Similarly, Octavia Hill (1893) expressed the view that 'We are educating, not a mechanic to practise manual work, not a lawyer whose intellect must be developed and mind stored with facts, not a physician who must gather knowledge and dispense advice, but a worker who, though she may need a certain manual skill, and clear intellect, and knowledge, is primarily a human being who may use manual and mental power for the help and blessing of numbers of families. That being so, all will depend on what she is . . .'

This devotion of the resources of personality was not, however, a straightforward, outright gift, though it assumed this character in some writings. Toynbee, for instance, conceived of social work essentially as a reparative act, but the general view emphasised the demand that the social worker ought to make on the client for his own good. The following extract illustrates the form this might take (Barnett, 1918, p. 210).

Mrs. Barnett is in a workhouse talking to 'a sullen girl'.

'It is my birthday on Tuesday,' I said. No reply. 'Don't you want to give me a present?' Long silence and then— 'I ain't got nothing to give nobody' was grunted out. 'You have something you can give me which I want very much,' I said. Silence. 'Won't you give it me?' Silence. Then curiosity awoke, and she sulkily asked, 'What is it?' 'You can give me your promise that if I take you out of here, you will never enter the work-house again.' Silence, this time unbroken until I had to go, but on Tuesday the eagerly looked-for letter was there, and the given promise was faithfully kept.

The principle of 'give but demand' or of 'reciprocity' was central to the social work of C. S. Loch and others and marks a feature distinguishing their social work from their more 'psychiatric' successors. As Urwick (1930) remarked, 'What place is there for the full principle of reciprocity in a science which converts all our reforming zeal into the ancillary of specialised medical treatment?' Given these two primary characteristics of self-devotion and of demand of the other, in what way did the early social workers des-cribe their relationships with those they were trying to help? To some the idea of friendship seemed appropriate. The Settlement movement, for example, was seen by many of its supporters as providing them with the opportunity to act as 'a cultivated friend' (Addams, 1893) to people deprived of culture and of contact with any but their own class. The notion of 'friendly visiting' as a distinct branch of social work was strongly upheld in the last decades of the nineteenth and the first of the twentieth century, and Mary Richmond (1903) devoted a book to the subject.

We should be willing to listen patiently to the home maker's troubles, and should strive to see the world from her point of view, but at the same time we should help her to take a cheerful and courageous tone. One unfail-ing help, when our poor friends dwell too much upon their own troubles, is to tell them ours. Here, too, in-direct suggestion is powerful. The wife, in her attitude toward husband and children, will unconsciously imitate our own attitude toward them. (p. 71-2)

The idea of friendship has been used fitfully in social work ever since those early days. The Charity Organisation Society talked significantly of 'watchful friendliness', adding to their statement of aims in 1910 that those influenced by this 'may greatly better the conditions of life in their homes and families'. Other writers referred to 'friendly but serious' (Hale, 1943) conversations with clients or to the fact that 'In every interview there is time for the ordinary chatter and manners of social life and a need for them in that they constitute the recognised indication of friendly intention . . . .' (Snelling, 1947) More recently, the notion of casework as friendship has been revived. One worker (Sheppard, 1964) has described a case in which she became a friend to her 'client', pointing out that she had to be a 'good friend', more in the sense perhaps of 'perfection' than of effectiveness. The worker suggests that

'one of the most valuable tools the social worker has ever had is that her position allows her to sit down with her 'client' in a *friendly* way, or as person to person. . . . A professional casework relationship is considered to differ from a friendship in that in friendship two people each expect to receive from and give to the other, whereas in the professional relationship the first consideration is to the client. Yet most of us probably have amongst our personal friends one who gives more to us than we to him, and one to whom we give more. But we still consider this person our friend.

How far are the terms 'friendship', 'friendly' and so on appropriately used in social work? Initially, the term covered the relationships established between social workers and clients with considerable strain. A work like *Neighbours and Friends* (Loane, 1910) for example, demonstrates a superiority and a conscious use of manipulation of the interaction to serve the worker's undeclared intention, which are hard to reconcile with 'friendship'. Sometimes the apparent strain between friendship and the worker's declared aim of impartiality was recognised: 'I think we have hardly the right to help a man until we have got, in some degree at least, to like him and understand him . . . on the other hand, we must not make favourites.' (Walrond, 1893) At other times social workers were only too well aware of what seemed to be the gap between themselves and those they should 'befriend'.

> And our way of looking at things, which can never be the way of those with whom we deal, however sympathetically we may enter into their troubles, however much knowledge we may have of the conditions in which they live; we can never see as they see, just because we stand outside the muddle of emotions, tendencies, scraps of experience . . . which make up the sum of another man's life. (A C.O.S. Secretary, 1926)

The present-day social worker does not think in such terms, and the application of the idea of friendship to contemporary social work appears more plausible. Yet the idea is not easily applied. This is partly because friendship is a complex notion about which it is easy to disagree. A study of the sociology of friendship (Beck and Useem, 1942) noted that 'there is no general consensus as to the meaning of the term friendship. To some it signifies an ease of companionship, an exchange of confidences without fear of misunderstanding, censure or exposure. To others, it means an individual on whom one can depend in time of crisis.' On some definitions of friendship certainly there would be little point in referring to casework as friendship. Oakeshott (1962, p. 244), for instance, characterises friendship in terms of enjoyment.

> Friends and lovers are not concerned with what can be made out of each other, but only with the enjoyment of one another. A friend is not somebody one trusts to behave in a certain manner, who has certain useful qualities, who holds acceptable opinions; he is somebody who evokes interest, delight, unreasoning loyalty, and who (almost) engages contemplative imagination. The relationship of friends is dramatic, not utilitarian.

If casework was equated with friendship in this way of regarding the term, the financing of casework services would have to be undertaken by the Arts Council.

Other commentators suggest that the description of social work as friendship conceals an essential element of deception. Winch (1958, p. 123), for example, takes exception to the view expressed in a popular text on the social services that it is the duty of a social worker to establish a relationship of friendship with her clients, but that she must never forget that her first duty is to the policy of the agency by which she is employed. 'Now that is a debasement of the notion of friendship as it has been understood, which has excluded this sort of divided loyalty, not to say double-dealing.'

These difficulties in the description of the social worker as the client's friend suggests that the idea of social work as friendship requires systematic treatment. This could proceed in three related ways. Firstly, we should make a persistent attempt to distinguish the role of friendship from a 'friendly way' of playing other roles. Thus, a person selecting someone for a job, a policeman, a father talking to his son, could in all circumstances be described as pursuing their tasks in a friendly rather than a formal way. Their 'friendliness' helps them to perform particular tasks, but it is in no way essential for the performance. Failure to observe this distinction has resulted in a muddled treatment of the topic in social work.

Secondly, we would extend our understanding of social work by enquiring into certain negative aspects of friendship. We should ask how we came to speak of the end of a friendship: under what circumstances we are justified in saying a friendship has been betrayed, and so on. We could then consider if and to what extent these situations resemble those in which we speak of the end of a casework relationship or the failure of one of both parties to observe the norms of their relationship. This is not an enquiry for which we can at present expect much help from past empirical observation. 'Few systematic studies of the formation of friends also incorporate materials on the disruption of friendship.' (Zazarsfield and Merton, 1954)

Thirdly, we should consider border-line cases. Early social workers spoke of friendship, but also of 'neighbours' and, quite insistently, of 'fellow-citizenship'. The list could now be extended to include 'acquaintances' and 'relatives' from amongst whom it is now possible to choose those with whom one will develop a special degree of intimacy. These terms could be said to be on the border with friendship. Reflection about their similarities with and differences from friendship will help us to discern the ways in which social work can be described as the offer of friendship.

Social worker as therapist

The identification of social work as a kind of therapy, usually a psychoanalytic one, arises from two distinct sources. There are those inside and outside the profession of social work who argue that 'psychiatric' influences have distorted what they see as genuine social work activity. Thus, Macrae (1940) points to 'a great deal of semi-Freudian prurience and false science substituting for administrative advice and economic aid'; whilst much earlier (1930) a reviewer of Robinson's *A Changing Psychology in Social Case-Work* suggested that 'in case-work personality tends to be studied as such. The case-worker is more disposed to regard his client as a potential neurotic or psychopathic than as a potential "Civis Romanus".' Others have argued that what has come to be called, somewhat mistakenly, 'the psychiatric deluge' (Woodroofe, 1962) has quenched the fires of social reform. Others have examined the implications for social work practice of what are described as the two Freudian concepts of 'social adjustment' and 'psychological determinism'. Many social workers, however, acknowledge an indebtedness to psychoanalytic ideas in the improvement of their practice, and define themselves as therapists rather than experts in the social services, or reformers.

The fact that the identification of social work as a therapy is seen, on the one hand, as somewhat scandalous, and, on the other, as an advance, complicates the task of assessing how far what is claimed or derided develops our understanding of the nature of social work. We need to distinguish the several questions that can be asked about the relationship between social work and psychoanalytic therapy. In this section, we shall be concerned with three of these questions: what, if anything, distinguishes psycho-analytic therapy from social casework; how do social workers use the ideas derived from psychoanalysis; do they implicitly import into their work from psychoanalytic therapy certain emphases which require examination? In pursuing this particular set of questions we shall not be centrally interested in whether psychoanalytic influence has been detrimental nor even in possible alternative theories. The focus will be provided by the attempt to discern what the pursuit of the questions tells us of the nature of social work.

Differentiation between therapy and casework

In this section it is assumed that no question arises of distinguishing casework from psychoanalysis, since the free association necessary for the latter is not *enforced as a rule* in the former. What has been seen as problematic is the identity of casework in relation to a range of therapies which fall short of psychoanalysis, whilst still emphasising the persistent scrutiny of the relationship between 'patient' and 'therapist'. It is, for instance, commonly suggested that the social worker as therapist does not aim at 'basic personality change'. This looks like an act of restraint: the social worker or someone else *could* entertain such an aim, but chooses not to. The disclaimer, however, contains very little information, since it rarely conveys any notion of what is to count as 'basic personality change', and certainly some analysts would emphasise the analysis of a patient rather than any change that could be described as 'basic'. Rieff (1960, p. 72) has aptly suggested that 'granting an occasional opportunity for opposing reality, the Freudian therapy remains mainly a tutorial in the managerial virtues of prudence and compromise'.

This instance of a fairly common way of distinguishing psychoanalytic therapy from social work indicates the importance of two questions in any attempt at differentiation: in what terms is the distinction made, and what criteria are suggested for using particular descriptions within the terminology adopted. Thus, the above differentiation is made in terms of the different objectives of therapy, and social workers are said to pursue objectives that can be described as falling short of 'basic personality change', whatever is intended by such a phrase. It is particularly important to recognise the terminology employed, because this can often lead to pertinent questions that would otherwise remain concealed. Talking, for instance, in the terminology of 'objectives' should lead to questions concerning the different viewpoints from which objectives could be described. Are the objectives those that could be described as 'theoretical' or are they those actually entertained by practitioners? Answers to this question could lead to a consideration of how the objectives of practitioners are discovered, since someone could properly be said 'to know what he is doing/what he is at' without being able to give any account, let alone a correct one, of 'what he was aiming at'. Finally, in an activity like therapy in which so much seems to depend on interaction it seems unlikely that we could be entirely satisfied with an account of objectives from one side of the relationship only. We are likely to advance the understanding of any distinctions between therapy and casework by examining the objectives of patients and clients as well as of therapists and social workers. In this way we shall be able to correct the view that casework is 'a form of quasi-captive psychotherapy done in the name of advancing the professionalisation of social work but largely in ignorance of the attitudes and definitions of one of the two participants.' (Kuhn, 1962)

The importance of the twofold attention to the kind of terminology and to asking what counts as any particular description within the terminology, could be illustrated in any of the attempts to distinguish social work from psychotherapy. Take, for example, the suggestion that 'social workers do not interpret unconscious material, but they may interpret pre-conscious material'. The most helpful response to this is not simple acceptance or denial, but, recognising that the terminology concerns activity rather than objectives, to consider if this kind of territorial demarcation actually works, and to ask what counts as an interpretation. If, as Farrell (1962) maintains, an interpretation is not a hypothesis that might be true or false, but an instrument for producing changes regarded as desirable, we cannot assume without further argument that changes desirable in the course of therapy are identical with those required in social work.

This kind of questioning approach could be adopted with regard to all the attempted differentiations of social work from psychotherapy, but rather than illustrate this exhaustively, it is worthwhile considering at this stage why the distinction is important. Surely, it could be argued, nothing very much hangs on the decision that social work is or is not a therapy. Some social workers describe their work in a way that appears to make any differentiation from therapy futile. Can we not simply say that some practise therapy and some do not? Unfortunately, the issue cannot be left like that, since we are faced with questions concerning their rightful practice as therapists. To talk of 'therapy' is to think in terms of a particular kind of training, of a certain kind of treatment programme, of the practice of certain techniques, and of particular definitions of 'patient' and 'therapist'. These terms cannot readily be used in a description of social work.

It is, however, important to bear in mind the different

reasons for which we might wish to distinguish social work from therapy, and to try to match explanation with reason. If, for instance, we are concerned with the protection of clients from amateur therapy it is difficult to see what is being ruled out when the worker is told it is not his function 'to attempt to explore the depths of the mind' (Ferard and Hunnybun, 1962, p. 5). If we are anxious to explore the existence of a special role for social work it is clearly frustrating to see social work distinguished from therapy only within a psychoanalytic terminology, for instance, in terms of the differential handling of the transference neurosis.

The use of psychoanalytic ideas

A distinction is often made between the explanatory theories of psychoanalysis (e.g. infantile sexuality) and the technical devices used to achieve particular results (e.g. free association, dream interpretation). Social workers have often voiced their conviction in the usefulness of the former, whilst declining to use the latter. This immediately and usefully illustrates one of the main arguments of this section, namely that in using psychoanalytic conceptions (or in this case a model of the relationship between such conceptions) crucial mistakes are sometimes made. The model of psychoanalysis as science and as method insufficiently emphasises the character of psychoanalysis as a technique with a highly developed technology. As Freud wrote (1909), '. . . a psychoanalysis is not an impartial scientific investigation, but a therapeutic measure. Its essence is not to prove anything, but merely to alter something.'

In general psychoanalytic concepts seem to function in

three ways. Firstly, they are borrowed in what appears to be a fairly straightforward way. In this case two sorts of question arise. The usage of the term by social workers may or may not accord with psychoanalytic theorising, and the term may or may not add something to descriptions in more day-to-day language. The term 'ego', for example, is extremely economical and hence not easily replaceable by a less theoretical description, but it seems often to be vulgarised by social workers. Judgements are recorded concerning a client's 'ego strength' without a full appreciation of the complexity of such a statement. As Fenichel (1955) observed, '. . . there can be an ego that at the same time fulfils one function very reliably and well, and another badly . . . it may well permanently repress instinctual drives (i.e. be strong in relation to the id) because, say, it has exaggerated anxiety (i.e. is weak in relation to the outer world).' Similarly, the use by social workers of the term 'super-ego' as synonymous with 'conscience' tends to blunt the cutting edge of the term in psychoanalytic theory and to oversimplify the ancient and complex language of 'conscience'.

Secondly, social workers think of themselves as adopting what is described as 'a psychoanalytic approach'. This again leads to a consideration of two topics, the possible drawbacks to this kind of variegated theoretical basis, and the assumptions that accompany an analytical approach. The latter will be considered in the following section, and here it is necessary only to call attention to two aspects of the former, the confusion in social work education and the hindrance to further exploration. As Boehm (1959) observed in his study of American social work curricula, 'it is not always clear which branch of Freudian theory is being advocated and sometimes the impression has been created that a variety of classic concepts are thrown together with concepts drawn from various neo-Freudian and psycho-anthropological schools of thought. Unless these various theoretical pieces are put together consistently, they cannot fail to confuse the student. . . .' It could be argued that clarity is a less desirable goal than effectiveness, and that the differences between concepts and theories are of minor importance provided the 'over-all' conception works. Yet this kind of argument frustrates any exploration of what it is that 'works', and how it can be made to work more effectively.

An exploration of the psychoanalytic concepts used in social work education and practice could take one of two forms. The first would consist of a systematic listing and analysis of the various terms used, tracing them to their theoretical source with the aid of a work like Monroe (1957). Such a procedure would remove some of the confusion and also test the commonly made assertion that 'It is easy to show how an insight or a new explanatory concept in therapy is passed down the line, usually starting with psychoanalytical reappraisals, and ending with the social casework theoreticians translating the thing into the idiom of the social caseworkers.' (Halmos, 1965) Alternatively—and this will be the approach adopted in this section—the attempt could be made to examine what difference a non-eclectic psychological theory made to the description of social work practice. In the following pages we shall discern the kind of social work that seems to follow from a psychology that can be classified as broadly psychoanalytical, that of Otto Rank. This psychology formed the basis of practice for one particular group of social workers in America, the so-called Functional School. This school and the debate in which they engaged with what has been called the Diagnostic School has been strangely neglected in Britain where the lack of strong controversy is such a significant feature in the development of social work. The differences between the Schools will be discussed here not with the intention of deciding that one of the two was somehow 'right', but of illustrating the implications of a particular psychological theory for the kinds of difficulty about which social workers have argued. One way of illuminating the nature of social work is to examine just that topic.

Otto Rank, originally an adherent of Freud, broke with him and established his own school of psychotherapy. This rests basically on a rather obscure view of 'the will', and on the idea of life as a problem of growth between the two polarities of dependence and independence. The social work teacher who contributed most to the use of Rankian psychology, Jessie Taft, wrote (quoted Smalley, 1967, pp. 82-3)

> The two basic needs that form the two poles of the psychological growth process are the need for dependence on the other, as it is first experienced in the oneness of the uterine relationship, and the opposing need for the development of self-dependence as the goal of movement towards adulthood. The two are never divorced in living, and it is on their essential conflict and interaction that we rely for the dynamic that keeps the individual moving to correct the imbalance that exists and must exist at any given moment in his use of himself.

The individual is described as possessing an inborn will towards individuation and autonomy, and the self is the result of the creative use of inner and outer resources. The emphasis on all circumstances as opportunities resembles the earlier approach of C. S. Loch, the Bosanquets and others.

The Rankian psychology stresses growth which takes place through relationships, through a movement of the self towards and away from particular people. As the self moves into a new relationship the individual 'projects' his need upon the other. ('Project' is used here in the sense of appropriating a psychological object in self-interest, and not in the Freudian sense as a mechanism for disowning and discarding unwanted feelings, etc.) The satisfaction of the need by the other creates a union between the two persons, but because union in any complete sense is impossible in reality separation inevitably follows. The person can use this separation constructively by making the reality limits his own (i.e. by accepting and using them) or by striving for the infantile union, for complete unity at the pre-natal level. (Kasius ed., 1950)

What kind of social work does this psychological theory lead to? Rank himself did not directly apply his ideas to social work, but a number of social work teachers, particularly Taft and Robinson, did. In this context the social worker saw himself as aiming at the release of innate capacity, and as participating in a relationship in which the present was more important than the past and whose final state was essentially unpredictable. This could be contrasted with the Diagnostic School who emphasised differential diagnosis and treatment of conditions judged to be pathological. The Functionalists emphasised the notion of the helping process, whereas the Diagnosticians could refer to social work method as a repertoire of interventive acts on the part of the worker. (Smalley, p. 25)

We can see, then, in this example that it could be said 'to make a difference' if a social worker adopts a Rankian as opposed to a Freudian approach, but that the difference is more obvious in terms of a description of roles than in terms of the use of clearly distinguished theories that attempt to explain behaviour. And yet the most important contribution of the Functional School has not so far been mentioned, namely the concept of agency function, from which their name derives. This does not derive from the psychology of Rank, though it is discussed in his terminology, and it provides both the best means and the justification for distinguishing casework from therapy. The concept refers to the purpose for which an agency has been created. 'The use of an agency function (or purpose in action by the social worker gives focus, context and direction to a specific helping process and assures its social responsibility. . . . It contributes to the psychological helpfulness of the process as well.' (Smalley, p. 104) The social worker operates through relationships established between himself and his clients, but the function of the agency is always a third factor in the situation for participant and observer alike, helping the client to make decisions rather than enter treatment and, as it were, connecting client and worker with the wider society.

The crucial factor in distinguishing therapy from social work lies in the role of the social worker, in his 'connection' with the wider society that differs significantly from that of the therapist. It is his connection that the Functionalists have helpfully emphasised. It still requires elaboration, however. It is not without interest, for instance, that earlier writings from this School suggest that emphasis on 'the relationship' may have consequences that are not universally considered desirable. Robinson (1930) saw a conflict between 'the social welfare of the client versus the relationship between the worker and the client; the one determined by an undefined but active norm varying with the worker's standard and background, the other indeterminate, dynamic, often *subversive* of social norms'. (Italics not original) Later formulations seem to stress the basic compatibility between what are termed the needs of the individual client and the needs of society as interpreted in the function of particular agencies. This cannot simply be accepted as a basic proposition.

'Psychoanalytic' assumptions

It has been suggested that the use of specific psychoanalytic theories by social workers encourages the operation of assumptions that are inimical to social work values. This view receives particular attention in the work of Keith-Lucas (1962). He sees psychoanalytic theories as helping to move society away from a theocentric view of man towards one which he describes as humanistic-positivist-utopian. This view supposes that the primary purpose of society is to fulfil man's material and emotional needs. If these needs are met man will attain maturity, and most of his and society's problems will be solved, but man is hampered by circumstances outside his control. These circumstances can be manipulated by those with sufficient knowledge, hence man and society are perfectible. In particular Keith-Lucas is concerned with the shift in social work from help to control, which he sees as one of the consequences of the adoption of psychoanalytic theories. He points to the prevalent rationalisation 'that influence and persuasion do not involve the imposition of standards in the same way as do command and exhortation'. (Keith-Lucas, 1962)

How can this kind of argument be developed in a way that will enrich our understanding of social work? Firstly, we should recognise that there are various kinds of assumption: the more 'basically' one searches the more vacuous are likely to be the results. Thus, it has been suggested that a basic assumption of social work is that man is knowable. What requires examination are the logical and empirical connections between social work and psychoanalytic theories. The ideas that Keith-Lucas propounds as humanist, positivist and utopian are not logically entailed by psychoanalytic theories, so that one can deny these ideas and still hold to psychoanalytic theories without contradiction. Secondly, statements about control require careful examination, especially if social work as a 'helping process' is to be defined by the way it differs from a 'controlling process'. For instance, the suggestion in the above quotation that influence and persuasion involve the imposition of standards in the same way as command and exhortation tends to conglomerate and treat as the same the different activities of influencing, persuading, commanding and exhorting. The same kind of blurring occurs in the treatment Halmos (1965) accords to what he terms 'the myth of non-directiveness'. He seems to suggest that the myth is exploded because of the simple fact of the therapist's undeniable influence on the patient. But there are many kinds of influence, of which direction is only one. Thirdly, we should analyse the notion of a helping process. Is this, for example, a more helpful description of social work than that of 'loving' recently propounded (Halmos 1965)? Or is it not liable to the same criticism? As 'loving' obscures differences between the love of a man for his friend, a son for his father and a man for his wife, so 'helping' prevents our seeing the different criteria which enable us to judge when a man has helped his friend, his wife, his neighbour and his son.

7
Summary

This book will have been misunderstood if it is seen as yet another admonition to social workers to 'be more precise' in their use of terms. Indeed, if the argument of the book has been followed the reader will by now be considering what meaning can be attached to such general advice. 'Precision' only has meaning within a particular context, and statements can be judged 'precise' or otherwise only with a prior recognition of the kind of precision demanded by the language in which the context is given. Poetic statements, historical statements and many other kinds of proposition could all be described as precise, but there is no general criteria of precision they all meet. Similarly, when social workers are encouraged 'to be critical', they cannot see what is being required of them unless they are also given the set of ideas within which they could exercise a critical faculty.

The present work has aimed at sketching in outline some of the ideas and concepts helpful in understanding what kind of activity social work is. It does not give a definitive answer to this question, but instead raises new kinds of questions that seem more rewarding if initially more complex. The search for a satisfactory idea of the nature of social work has proceeded so far largely in terms of *a priori* definitions. International conferences on social work appear to thrive on this kind of activity, but they have produced little that is fruitful. This book has been based on the assumption that more returns are likely to accrue from a study of the language social work practitioners and teachers use. Thus, we have been concerned in this book with the attempt to discover some of the meanings that can be attached to the 'generic' and the 'specific' elements in social work, and with the extent to which it is helpful to analyse social work practice into an activity that takes place in a number of different 'settings'. The analysis has been conducted in a way that gives these terms their full weight and the aim has not been to belittle social work or social work theorising by saying that social workers do such good practical or moral work it is unfortunate that they hide it under the bushel of either professional status seeking or scientism.

The language of social work also contains many references to ideas outside its own boundaries, which are, in any case, very ill-defined. Thus, we have seen that social work has been described as a kind of therapy, a sort of friendship, or an applied science. Social workers in their daily practice talk of and use 'the social history'; they see themselves as 'diagnosing' and 'treating'. Many of these ideas and terms refer to disciplines other than social work, or to problems and processes that social workers may share with others. This book has argued that these references and similarities should be exploited, and that we should regard them not as so much embroidery but as tools for work. In this way some of the narrow circularity of social work argument can be broken into, and social workers will be at the beginning of a demonstration that their activity can, to use a phrase of Cowling, (1963, p. 24) 'bear the weight of sustained intelligence'.

In the present work we have been considering the terms social workers use and how their language compares with that of other disciplines. Yet it should not be envisaged that an approach which systematically looks outside the boundaries of social work will thereby produce definitive answers to problems within them. A comparison of the language of social work with other languages will, if the argument of this book is correct, always be worthwhile, but will rarely settle any issue in social work. There are two reasons for this. Firstly, what is complex and controversial in social work will often have controversial parallels in other disciplines. Thus, whether or not social work can be described as 'scientific' can be paralleled with a similar question in regard to history or literary criticism. Secondly, whilst it is always productive to learn to speak a language and reference to languages other than that of social work seems essential to an understanding of social work, the rules governing a language are not of supreme importance. As Oakeshott has said (1966) 'Art and conduct, science, philosophy and history, these are not modes of thought defined by rules; they exist only in personal explorations of territories only the boundaries of which are subject to definition.'

This book has been devoted to some studies in the language of social work, with the aim of encouraging further exploration. Its tone might be described as sceptical but this seems more respectful of the activity of social work than optimistic statements about the nature of social work propounded by commonly accepted authorities. The present study seeks to question the credentials of such authorities and the confident assertions made in many social work texts. It seeks to encourage a reflective consideration of social work activity in the light of ideas and concepts more highly developed than those to be found in social work itself. But it does not seek to replace one set of authorities by another.

Suggestions for further reading

Since the approach adopted and advocated in this book is a new one, at least as far as social work is concerned, there is no extensive literature to which reference can be made. The suggestions for reading which follow are in two parts: social work texts that seem to show clearly the kinds of proposition in social work that call for the reflective activity advocated in this book; secondly, works from other fields that could help to sustain and make profitable such an exercise. Works in this second group are not to be seen as a source of ready-made solutions, but as one way of helping us to recognise some important problems in social work for what they are.

Social work texts

There are a number of these which can be used as sources for current social work concepts and ideas. Biestek (1961) has written a text that is widely used in Britain, and Ferard and Hunnybun (1962) can be studied as illustrative of the influence of psychoanalytic ideas. Works by Young-husband (1964), Heywood (1964), and Monger (1964) also

provide accounts of casework that could be usefully ana-
lysed. In America texts by Perlman (1957) and Hamilton
(1940) can serve the same purpose. The analysis could
proceed in one of two ways. It could be conducted, as it
were, horizontally across authors. For example, one could
study formulations of casework principles in different
authors to discover whether the same principles were
always in evidence and, more significantly, whether the
authors were using 'principle' in the same way. Alternatively, a single text could be taken for systematic study.
As an illustration of this approach the rest of this section
will be concerned with a preliminary discussion of one of
the texts already mentioned (Perlman, 1957).

This text is clearly written and has gained considerable
popularity in this country as well as in America. The preliminary analysis will be discussed under the headings
Perlman herself uses of Person, Place, Problem and Process.
Under each of these headings significant propositions will
be identified and discussed.

Person. Early in the book Perlman faces the problem that
any systematic treatment of social work assumes or asserts
ideas about human nature. She states her view that 'The
person's behaviour has this purpose and meaning: to gain
satisfactions, to avoid or dissolve frustration, and to maintain his balance in movement'. (p. 7) This illustrates the
importance of differentiating between kinds of statement.
It claims to be an explanation of human behaviour, but
unlike true explanations, it cannot be conclusively tested;
it is a statement of general attitude, not a hypothesis. As a
statement of general attitude, however, it can be discussed
and appraised. One of the grounds of appraisal will be the
extent to which it is compatible with the rest of casework

theory. I would argue that Perlman's statement is open to the usual objections to hedonism (e.g. the confusion between the purpose of an action and the feeling that accompanies the attainment of that purpose) and has deterministic undertones that do not blend happily with other values of casework. There is, in fact, in her book a clear and sustained acknowledgment, on the one hand, of the rational nature of human action and, on the other, occasional but contradictory references to a casual view of human behaviour. Perlman does not resolve this conflict between a model of a man pursuing purposes more or less appropriate by means more or less fitting and that of man 'driven', 'propelled', and 'pulled' by internal and external forces.

Of the other propositions which Perlman makes concerning the person, limitation of space only permits discussion of her 'conception of human life as being in itself a problem-solving process, a continuous change and movement' (p. 53), and her view that a person's behaviour is shaped by the major social roles he carries (p. 22).

The first conception has a profound effect on several of the components of casework; it seems to justify Perlman's view that the whole is different from the sum of its parts (p. 5), that a diagnosis is more than a list of factors and that in a relationship problems are the result of the interaction of both partners (p. 14). Incidentally it is also held responsible for the difficulty of defining casework, as if a dynamic subject matter somehow necessitated a dynamic definition (p. 3, p. 151). General assertions about dynamic interaction are basic assumptions which cannot be tested; they represent a general point of view, but one which has technological implications. These technological implications can, of course, be tested within the field of casework. Such an implication would be, for example, that casework with a marital problem will fail unless the contribution of each partner to the problem is considered. It is in principle possible to test this assertion and others like it.

The concepts of role and status are defined, of course, in sociology, but they may be used in casework for descriptive purposes, a short-hand way of referring to several features of behaviour. In so far, however, as these concepts are used as part of an explanation of behaviour it seems likely that validation will come from sociological research outside the field of casework. Perlman's proposition that behaviour is 'both shaped and judged by the expectations he and his culture have invested in the status and major social roles he carries' is partly a hypothesis for such sociological investigation and partly tautological—if 'roles' *mean* partly at any rate, expectation, then people must be judged in accordance with role (i.e. expectation).

The place. In this section a distinction will be made between classifications and values.

Classifications vary in importance. Some are questions of terminology with no ramifications outside the initial decision. Thus, Perlman's classification of agencies by source of support, source of professional authority and special function is clear, necessary and adequate, and 'self-contained'. Other decisions carry far-reaching implications. Perhaps the most important of these is the decision to call the caseworker a professional person (p. 51). Once this has been accepted it is assumed that casework possesses all the attributes commonly observed in present-day professions. It thus becomes possible to speak of the authority of professional knowledge (p. 69) without having to justify the claim of 'knowledge'. There is nothing, of course, to prevent caseworkers from aspiring to professional ideals, but they must meanwhile in order to achieve professional status, justify their actions and attitudes by other means than simply calling them professional. The small amount of research into the perception of social casework by other professions and lay people suggests that the identity of casework is obscure and its claim to professional status recognised generally only by caseworkers.

Perlman makes an important formulation concerning the function of the social agency: 'The social agency is an organisation fashioned to express the will of a society or some group in that society as to social welfare.' (p. 43) This may well represent a sound view, but it is clearly a value judgement from which she attempts to derive empirical hypotheses concerning the perception of the client (he sees the agency 'as the expression of society's intent towards him and others like him'. (p. 44). Her view that 'an agency embodies a society's decision to protect its members', does not explain the rise of such minority groups as the Pacifist Service Unit in England during the last war, and cannot begin to bear the weight of any deduction. To suggest that the caseworker's authority somehow rests upon society's warrant to social agencies is an unjustified interpretation of function in terms of purpose. Her position would seem to require restatement in empirical terms (how clients in fact perceive agencies) and in terms of explicit values.

Problem. The assertions Perlman makes about 'problem' are again of different kinds. For example, she suggests that 'whatever the nature of the problem the person brings to the social agency, it is always accompanied, and often complicated by the problem of being a client'. (p. 37) This assertion seems to Perlman to be justified by the experience of caseworkers. In fact the proposition is an untested hypothesis; it looks as if it may be true, but can we claim to *know*? Only when this descriptive fact about clients has been established will it be possible to investigate the different explanatory hypotheses that Perlman gives to account for the fact—cultural factors, feelings of uncertainty and powerlessness, etc.

These are problems of description and explanation that could be solved within the casework discipline. There are, however, other assertions which do not appear so obviously testable. For example, 'any problem which a person encounters has both an objective and subjective significance'. The only way in which this could be tested is to restate the proposition in terms of a basic assumption of the general importance of emotional factors and to test the technological implications of this restatement. For example, 'the caseworker should relate consistently to the client's feelings'. (p. 143)

It has always proved difficult for writers on casework to state clearly those problems that come within the scope of casework. Perlman suggests that they are problems that affect or are affected by social functioning (p. 28); maladjustments in vital social roles (p. 25); or threats to social comfort and adequacy. Her attempts to justify these suggestions on the grounds that 'it helps the caseworker chart his focus, his work plan and his goals' (p. 29) seem merely to repeat that these matters are the caseworker's concern. The proper justification of the scope of casework would seem to be partly logical, partly social, partly political and partly a matter for research : what are the implications for practice of the training given; what do clients expect and benefit from; what is politically recognised in terms of grants for student training, registration etc.; what in fact can casework achieve?

Process. Perhaps the most important technological decision in casework is, what kind of activity is it? Hamilton sees casework as 'treatment', Perlman as 'problem-solving' and each presents casework in terms of the logic of these concepts. The decision that casework is a problem-solving activity, for example, helps Perlman to justify her position in the diagnostic-functional conflict. Every problem-solving process necessitates diagnosis, therefore, the caseworker is in fact 'Diagnosing as he relates to another person in a purposeful, problem-solving activity' (p. 165).

Perlman stresses both the ordinary and orderly aspects of the method of casework; she is not under pressure to establish an elaborate catalogue of casework treatments. She refers, for example, to 'simple, natural communications' and to the process of diagnosis as 'the method of logical thinking we use every day'. (p. 179) There are, however, technical principles which she proposes for adoption—the caseworker should engage a person in working on his problems (because people learn by doing or because repeated exercises in problem-solving help to form habits of orderly thinking etc.); the caseworker 'stands for reality' ('the help offered is never that of evading society's demands', p. 155), and should 'give full acceptance to the expressed feeling but draw out and work over its opposite side'. (p. 154) These principles are all directly concerned with practice, but they derive from different sources. The first is based on a hypothesis of learning or of habitation; the second states a basic assumption; the third could be tested in casework practice, but could also depend on the prior acceptance of a psychological theory of opposites such as is presented in the work of Jung.

The aims or goals of casework, as Perlman indicates, are extremely difficult to elucidate. She usefully distinguishes the general goals of the profession ('our highest aspirations for human well-being', p. 201) from the goal for each single client. It would be preferable to see these general goals stated as values of high generality, since they do not represent any state of affairs that could be realised, and goals for each single client separated into long-term and short-term. But whatever the formulation adopted it is of considerable importance that some distinctions are introduced into what is one of the most vacuous areas of casework discussion. Perlman's general position seems to be that no 'static' goal is possible, but that in each individual case the goal should be 'to set and keep in motion' capacities for adaptation. In her view, the 'problem-solving means and the problem-solving ends are as one' (p. 203). This slightly mystical formation closes the major section of Perlman's book. It represents a position difficult to grasp and to justify, but it seems acceptable to Perlman mainly because it recognises one of her most important basic assumptions (that the human world is one of dynamic interaction) and because it leans heavily upon a theory of growth in which first place is given to the concepts of ego-psychology.

Other works

This is largely a question of personal choice: a number of texts, largely in philosophy or the philosophy of such disciplines as history, literature or sociology could help to sustain and develop curiosity about problems in social work. In this particular book Casey (1966) on literary criticism, Polanyi (1958) on scientific ideas, and Oakeshott

(1962, 1967) on different kinds of discourse have been found particularly fruitful. These and other works, however, should not be scanned with the hope that something useful will turn up. We should as it were, bring to a reading of these and similar works an active sense of puzzlement about one or other aspect of social work.

Thus the question often raised by social workers about the nature of their activity should not be taken at its face value and a ready-made solution sought in, say, a volume on the philosophy of science. Instead we could usefully reflect on the question, beginning to recognise that it is, to a degree, a strange question, since social workers have been practising social work for many years. What is the perplexity they evidently experience, what is it like? Does it resemble the situation in which a musician says 'I cannot make any sense of this piece of music, though I can read all the notes', or an actor says, 'I wonder if I have interpreted the role correctly; I think I will know when I have'. There are different kinds of perplexity, different explanations of behaviour, different kinds of intelligible discourse. Social work will establish a firm identity as the similarities of its operations with other activities and the differences from them are gradually established.

Bibliography

ADDAMS, J. (1893) 'The Subjective Necessity for Social Settlements' in *Philanthropy and Social Progress* ed. Addams, J., *et al.*, New York.

ANDERSON, A. (1964) 'Living Words', *Case Conference*, Vol. XI, No. 1, May, 1964.

BARNARD, F. M. (1965) *Herder's Social and Political Thought*, Oxford: Clarendon Press.

BARNETT, H. (1918) *Canon Barnett, His Life, Work and Friends*, London.

BARTLETT, H. (1959) 'The Generic—Specific Concept in Social Work Education and Practice', *Issues in American Social Work* ed. Kahn, A. J., New York: Columbia University Press.

(1961) *Analysing Social Work Practice by Fields*, New York: National Association of Social Workers.

BECKER, H. and USEEM, R. (1942) 'Sociological Analysis of the Dyad', *American Sociological Review*, VII, No. 1, February, 1942.

BIESTEK, F. (1961) *The Casework Relationship*, London: Allen & Unwin.

BILLINGSLEY, A. (1964) 'Bureaucratic and Professional Orientation Patterns', *Social Service Review*, Vol. XXXVIII, No. 4, December.

BISNO, H. (1952) *The Philosophy of Social Work*, Washington : Public Affairs Press.

BOEHM, W. W. (1959) The Social Casework Method in Social Work Education, Vol. X, *Curriculum Study*, Council of Social Work Education, U.S.A. 1959.

BOSANQUET, B. (1901) 'The Meaning of Social Work', *International Journal of Ethics*, Vol. XI, No. 3, 1901.

BOSANQUET, H. (1914) *Social Work in London, 1869-1912*, London : John Murray.

BOWERS, S. (1949) 'The Nature and Definition of Social Casework', *Social Casework*, XXX, Nos. 8, 9 & 10, October, November, December, 1949.

BOWLBY, J. (1958) 'Psycho-Analysis and Child Care' *Psycho-Analysis and Contemporary Thought*, ed. Sutherland, J., London : Hogarth Press.

BUTLER, B. (1962) 'Casework Jargon', *Case Conference*, Vol. VIII, No. 7, January, 1962.

CASEY, J. (1966) *The Language of Criticism*, London : Methuen.

COCKERILL, E., *et al.*, (1952) *A Conceptual Framework for Social Casework*, University of Pittsburgh Press.

COLERIDGE, S. T. (1917) *The Table Talk and Omnia*, London : Oxford University Press.

COLLEGE OF PRECEPTORS, *Report of a Conference on The Concept of Professional Status*, 1957.

CORNFORTH, M. (1965) *Marxism and Linguistic Philosophy*, London : Lawrence & Wishart.

A C.O.S. SECRETARY (1926) 'Failure', *Charity Organisation Quarterly*, January, 1926.

COWLING, M. (1963) *The Nature and Limits of Political Science*, London: Cambridge University Press.

DEVONS, E. (1961) 'Applied Economics—The Application of What?' in *The Logic of Personal Knowledge: Essays Presented to M. Polanyi*, London: Routledge & Kegan Paul.

DONNISON, D. V. and CHAPMAN, V. (1965) *Social Policy and Administration*, London: Allen & Unwin.

EATON, J. (1959) 'A Scientific Basis for Helping', *Issues in American Social Work* (ed. Kahn), New York: Columbia University Press.

FAATZ, A. (1953) *The Nature of Choice in Social Casework*, Durham, N.C.: University of North Carolina Press.

FARRELL, B. (1962) 'Criteria for a Psychoanalytic Interpretation', *Proceedings of the Aristotelian Society*, Supplementary Vol. XXXVI, 1962.

FENICHEL, OTTO (1955) 'Ego Strength and Ego Weakness', *Collected Papers*, Second Series, ed. Fenichel, H., and Rapaport, D., London: Routledge & Kegan Paul.

FERARD, M. and HUNNYBUN, N. (1962) *The Caseworker's Use of Relationships*, London: Tavistock Publications.

FORDER, A. (1966) *Social Casework and Administration*, London: Faber & Faber.

FREUD, S. (1909) 'Analysis of a Phobia in a five-year old boy', *Collected Papers*, Vol. III, 1909, London: Hogarth Press (1956-7).

GOLDBERG, E. M. (1963) 'Function and Use of Relationship in Psychiatric Social Work', *Relationship in Casework*, London: Association of Psychiatric Social Workers.

GOODE, W. (1966) 'Professions and Non-Professions', in

Professionalisation ed. Vollmer, H., and Mills, D., New York: Prentice Hall.

GOULDNER, A. (1956) 'Exploration in Applied Social Science', *Social Problems*, Vol. III, No. 3, January, 1956.

GRAY, B. KIRKMAN (1908) *Philanthropy and the State*, London: P. S. King.

GREENWOOD, E. (1955) 'Social Science and Social Work: a theory of their relationship', *Social Service Review*, XXIX, No. 1, March, 1955.

GRENE, M. (1961) 'The Logic of Biology' in *The Logic of Personal Knowledge: Essays Presented to M. Polanyi*, London: Routledge & Kegan Paul.

HALBERT, L. A. (1923) *What is Professional Social Work?* Kansas City: University of Kansas.

HALE, M., and S. (1943) *Social Therapy*, London.

HALMOS, P. (1965) *The Faith of The Counsellors*, London: Constable.

HAMILTON, G. (1940) *Theory and Practice of Social Casework*, New York: Columbia University Press.
(1949) 'Helping People—The Growth of a Profession' in *Social Work as Human Relations*, New York: Columbia University Press.

HAMPSHIRE, S. (1960) *Thought and Action*, London: Chatto & Windus.

HEYWOOD, J. (1964) *An Introduction to Teaching Casework Skills*, London: Routledge & Kegan Paul.

HILL, O. (1893) 'Trained Workers for the Poor', *Nineteenth Century*, January, 1893.

HOLLIS, F. (1955) 'Principles and Assumptions underlying Casework Practice', *Social Work*, XII, No. 2, April, 1955.
(1956) 'The Generic and Specific in Social Casework Re-examined', *Social Casework*, XXXVII, No. 5, May, 1956.

IRVINE, E. E. 'Transference and Reality in The Casework Relationship', *Relationship in Casework*, London: Association of Psychiatric Social Workers.

JEFFERYS, M. (1965) *An Anatomy of Social Welfare Services*, London: Michael Joseph, 1965.

JEHU, D. (1966) *Learning Theory and Social Work*, London: Routledge & Kegan Paul, 1966.

KADUSHIN, A. (1959) 'The Knowledge Base of Social Work', *Issues in American Social Work*, ed. Kahn, A. J., New York: Columbia University Press.

KARPF, J. (1931) *The Scientific Basis of Social Work*, New York: Columbia University Press.

KASIUS, C., ed. (1950) *A Comparison of Diagnostic and Functional Casework Concepts*, London: F.S.A.A.

KEITH-LUCAS, A. (1962) 'Psychoanalytic Thinking and the Relief of the Poor' in *Psychiatry and Responsibility*, ed. Shoeck, H., and Wiggins, J., New York: Van Nostrand, (1966) 'The Art and Science of Helping', *Case Conference*, Vol. XIII, No. 5, September, 1966.

KNEALE, W. & M. (1962) *Development of Logic*, London: Oxford University Press.

KUHN, M. (1962) 'The Interview and the Professional Relationship', *Human Behaviour and Social Processes*, ed. Rose, A. M., London: Routledge & Kegan Paul.

LAZARSFIELD, P. F., and MERTON, R. (1954) 'Friendship as Social Process', *Freedom and Control in Modern Society*, ed. Berger, M., *et al.*, New York: Van Nostrand & Co., 1954.

LEHRMAN, L. (1954) 'The Logic of Diagnosis', *Social Casework*, XXXV, No. 5, May, 1954.

LEONARD, P. (1966) 'Scientific Method in Social Work Education', *Case Conference*, Vol. XIII, No. 5, September, 1966.

LIPELES, J. (1956) 'Teaching Social Work in a Medical Setting', *Social Casework*, Vol. XXXVIII, No. 9, November, 1956.

LOANE, M. (1910) *Neighbours and Friends*, London: Edward Arnold.

LOCH, C. S. (1899) 'Christian Charity and Political Economy', *Charity Organisation Review*, November, 1899. (1910) *Charity and Social Life*, London: Macmillan.

MACADAM, E. (1914) 'The Universities and The Training of The Social Worker', *Hibbert Journal*, XII, 1914, p. 283-294.

MACINTYRE, A. (1967) *A Short History of Ethics*, London: Routledge & Kegan Paul.

MACPHERSON, C. (1965) *The Real World of Democracy*, Toronto: Canadian Broadcasting Corporation.

MACRAE, D. G. (1960) 'Between Science and the Arts', *Twentieth Century*, May, 1960.

MAYER, J., and ROSENBLATT, A. (1964) 'The Client's Social Context: Its Effect on Continuance in Treatment', *Social Casework*, Vol. XLV, No. 9, November.

MILES, T. R. (1966) *Eliminating the Unconscious*, London: Pergamon Press.

MILFORD CONFERENCE (1929) 'Generic and Specific'. A Report of the American Association of Social Workers.

MINISTRY OF HEALTH (1959) *Report of The (Younghusband) Working Party on Social Workers in Local Authority Health and Welfare Services*, London: H.M.S.O.

MINOGUE, K. (1963) *The Liberal Mind*, London: Methuen.

MONGER, M. (1964) *Casework in Probation*, London: Butterworths.

MONROE, R. (1957) *Schools of Psychoanalytic Thought*, London: Hutchinson.

OAKESHOTT, M. (1962) *Rationalism in Politics*, London: Methuen.

(1967) 'Learning and Teaching', *The Concept of Education*, ed. R. S. Peters, London: Routledge & Kegan Paul.

PERLMAN, H. (1957) *Social Casework: a Problem-Solving Process*, University of Chicago Press.

PERROW, C. (1965) 'Hospitals: Technology, Structure and Goals', *Handbook of Organisations* ed. March, J., New York: Rand McNally.

POLANYI, M. (1951) *The Logic of Liberty*, London: Routledge & Kegan Paul.

(1958) *Personal Knowledge*, London: Routledge & Kegan Paul.

POLLAK, O. (1951) 'Relationships between Social Science and Child Guidance Practice', *American Sociological Review*, Vol. XVI, No. 1, February, 1951.

POWER, M. (1956) 'Community Care—A New Service', *British Journal of Psychiatric Social Work*, Vol. III, No. 3, 1956.

RAPOPORT, L. (1960) 'In Defence of Social Work: An Examination of Stress in the Profession', *Social Service Review*, Vol. XXXIV, No. 1, March, 1960.

RATHBONE, W. (1867) *Method Versus Muddle in Charitable Work*, first published as *Social Duties in Benevolence and Public Utility*, London: Macmillan.

REYNOLDS, B. (1964) 'The Social Casework of an Uncharted Journey', *Social Work*, (U.S.A.), Vol. IX, 1964.

RICHARDS, I. (1924) *Principles of Literary Criticism*, London: Routledge & Kegan Paul.

RICHMOND, M. (1903) *Friendly Visiting Amongst the Poor*, London: Macmillan.

(1917) *Social Diagnosis*, New York: Russell Sage Foundation.

ROBINSON, V. (1930) *A Changing Psychology in Social Casework*, University of Pennsylvania Press.

ROBSON, W. (1966) *Critical Essays*, London: Routledge & Kegan Paul.

RYLE, G. (1967) 'Teaching and Training', *The Concept of Education*, ed. Peters, R. S., London: Routledge & Kegan Paul.

SHEPPARD, M. L. (1964) 'Casework as Friendship: A Long Term Contract with a Paranoid Lady', *British Journal of Psychiatric Social Work*, VII, No. 4, 1964.

SMALLEY, R. (1967) *Theory for Social Work Practice*, New York: Columbia University Press.

SMITH, H. G. (1964) 'Professional Training and Afterwards', *Case Conference*, XI, No. 1, 1964.

SNELLING, J. (1947) 'Some Notes on Hospital Interviewing', *Social Work*, Vol. IV, January, 1947.

A Socialist View of Social Work (undated) issued by Social Workers Group of the Socialist Medical Association.

STUDT, E. (1965) 'Fields of Social Work Practice: Organising Our Resources for more Effective Practice', *Social Work*, (U.S.A.), Vol. X, October, 1965.

THOMAS, G. (1909) *Social Work*, London: Longmans, Green.

TITMUSS, R. M. (1954) 'The Administrative Setting of the Social Services', *Case Conference*, I, No. 1, May, 1954.

(1965) 'The Relationship between Schools of Social Work, Social Research, and Social Policy', *Journal of Education for Social Work*, I, No. 1, Spring, 1965.

TOWLE, C. (1954) *The Learner in Education for the Professions*, University of Chicago Press.

URWICK, E. (1912) *The Philosophy of Social Progress*, London: Methuen.
(1930) 'Reciprocity', *Charitable Organisation Quarterly*, April, 1930.

VIDLER, A. (1964) *Social Catholicism 1820-1920*, London: S.P.C.K.

WALD, F., and LEONARD. R. (1966) 'Towards the Development of Nursing Practice Theory' in *A Sociological Framework for Patient Care*, ed. Folta, J., and Deck, E., New York: John Wiley.

WALROND, F. F. (1893) 'Co-operation and the Need of Trained Workers', *Charity Organisation Review*, February, 1893.

WINCH, P. (1958) *The Idea of a Social Science*, London: Routledge & Kegan Paul.

WOODHOUSE, D. (1962) 'Some Implications for Casework Practice and Training', *The Marital Relationship as a Focus for Casework*, London: Codicote Press.

WOOLF, V. (1953) *A Writer's Diary*, London: Hogarth Press.

WOODROOFE, K. (1962) *From Charity to Social Work*, London: Routledge & Kegan Paul.

WOOTTON, B. (1955) *Social Science and Social Pathology*, London: Allen & Unwin.

YOUNGHUSBAND, Y. (1951) *Social Work in Britain*, London: Carnegie United Kingdom Trust.
(1964) *Social Work and Social Change*, London: Allen & Unwin.